Witch Trials, Legends, and Lore of Maryland

Dark, Strange, and True Tales

William H Cooke

http://www.MarylandWitches.com

ISBN: 0-6155-8886-7
ISBN-13: 9780615588865

Dedication

To the staff and volunteers at the Maryland State Archives

Contents

Preface

There is something intriguing about the witch trials of old. The idea that a lawyer could stand up seriously in court and accuse someone of making a pact with the Devil or using witchcraft to cause injury to others and he could get a conviction and death sentence for the defendant as a result just seems odd and wrong to any modern reader.

When I wrote my book, *Justice at Salem : Re-examining the witch trials* (published in 2009), I attempted to get into the heads of the officials who prosecuted the alleged witches as well as the people who made the accusations. Looking at the events through their eyes, without the benefit of modern science, I attempted to appreciate as much as possible their perspective.

The idea of charging, convicting, and executing someone for witchcraft in the 17th century and before was perfectly reasonable to most people. It was not until the 18th century when a paradigm shift happened. Then in the English-speaking world witchcraft ceased to be considered a felony, but rather was considered a nuisance at worst.

Witches no longer practiced their black arts, but rather only *pretended* to practice them. Nothing had changed, except the minds of the people who wrote the laws. Witches could no longer bring death and destruction. People who called themselves witches or who called others witches were more likely to be considered mentally ill.

It should make one wonder how people in the future might look back at elements of our criminal justice system now and may well consider us just as misguided as the witch hunters.

The study of witches or people who were considered to be witches, in America, is not limited to Salem, Massachusetts, or even to New England. Laws against witchcraft existed in all the early English colonies. Maryland was no exception.

From the earliest days of Maryland history (after the arrival of the British settlers), laws against witchcraft were on the statute books. Later those laws were amended and repealed, as they were in England, but the superstitions and fears associated with witches continued long after.

Maryland has always been a place full of rich legends and stories, some of them involving witches. This book explains the historical accounts of early Marylanders who were alleged to be witches and their interactions with the law. It is also a record of the folklore, customs and later traditions involving witchcraft and related superstitions in Maryland, up until present day.

This has been an exciting project for me and I hope that you enjoy reading this book and gain a greater appreciation for the history and culture of Maryland. A very special thank you is due to the Maryland Archives, the University of Maryland College Park Library, Star Etheridge, and Conrad and Mary Bladey.

Chapter 1
The History of Witchcraft and the Founding of Maryland

Witchcraft, broadly defined, is perhaps the world's oldest religion. Magic and sorcery, whether used for good or ill, were believed to have been real and were a part of different cultures in the ancient world.

Witchcraft used for evil ends was expressly condemned in Hammurabi's Code,[1] the ancient Greeks and Romans persecuted suspected witches, and witchcraft was condemned, for any purpose, by the Hebrews.[2]

Prohibitions against the use of magic and sorcery continued in Christianity and persecutions of suspected witches took place across Europe, among Catholics and various Protestant sects.[3]

Witchcraft did in fact exist, although not in the more dramatic sense. No reasonable person would actually believe that witches flew around on brooms or indeed in any other way. They did not really raise storms[4], harm or kill others at a distance with magic, change forms, fornicate with any supernatural devil, or engage in any of the other paranormal activities that they were alleged to have taken part in.

However, people who called themselves witches existed and did say spells, make curses, and took part in other rituals with the intent to cause harm.[5] The mindset of the victim, if he or she believed in the power of the witch, could produce harm through psychosomatic means.[6] Witches might have also engaged in more natural methods of causing harm, such as poisoning people or livestock.[7] However, completely innocent people were often wrongly accused of such crimes.

Before the advent of modern science, when people lived in a world that was only explainable through supernatural means, the perceived power of witches was taken for granted and just as there were laws against common murderers, robbers, and burglars, so to it made sense to have laws against those who inflicted harm on others with the Devil's assistance. What was called witchcraft was a felony in England in the 17th century and thus generally punishable by death, absent executive clemency.

A book written by a Michael Dalton in the early 17th century titled *The Country Justice*, provided a guide to judicial officials, such as Justices of the Peace, regarding how witchcraft was then defined in law. A 1690 reprint of the earlier text defined the elements and consequences of witchcraft as follows:

1. Conjuration, or Invocation of any evil Spirit, for any intent, &c. or to be counselling or aiding thereto, is felony without benefit of Clergy. See Exod. 22.18. Deut. 18.11. & Lev. 20.27. §. 4.Conjuration.

2. To consult, covenant with, entertain, imploy, feed, or reward any evil Spirit, to or for any intent or purpose, is felony in such Offenders, their Aiders and Counsellors.

3. To take up any dead Body, or any part thereof, to be imployed or used in any manner of Witchcraft, is felony in such Offenders, their Aiders and Counsellors.

4. Also to use or practice Witchcraft, Enchantment, Charm or Sorcery, whereby any person shall be killed, pined or lamed in any part of their Body, or to be counselling or aiding thereto, is felony: By the ancient Common Law such Offenders were to be burned, Fit. 269. b. ' See the ' Law of

God against Witches, Exod. 22.18. and against such as seek to ' Witches and Wizards, Levit. 19.31. & 20.6.

5.   Also the second time to practise Witchcraft, &c. thereby to declare where any Treasure may be found, is felony.

6.   Or where any Goods lost or stollen may be found.

7.   Or where any Cattel or Goods shall be destroyed or impaired.

8.   Or to the intent to provoke any person to love.

9.   Or to the intent to hurt any person in their body, though it be not effected. All these are felony, sc. the second Offence, and without benefit of Clergy.[8]

Witchcraft even for so-called good purposes was prohibited, but it was far more serious if a person was injured or killed as a result, even on a first offense. The Witchcraft Act of 1604, which the text explains, took a hard line against all manner of witchcraft.[9] Just as in England, laws against witchcraft in 17th century America were also on the statute books. Either the settlers would have directly followed the English law or they followed their own acts, passed by their governments, that were guided by the 1604 Witchcraft Act. The English colonies and provinces did not blindly mirror the laws passed by the English Parliament, but engaged in their own self-government to a great degree.[10] Witchcraft though was not legal in any 17th century English colony.[11]

When one thinks of witchcraft in America, one often thinks first of Salem, the city where over one hundred people were arrested and nineteen people were hanged as convicted witches during to so-called hysteria of 1692.[12]

The history of witchcraft in the America goes beyond that time and place. Witchcraft allegations and superstitions played a role along the Chesapeake. The original English settlers to America brought with them all of their old superstitions and beliefs and that included beliefs about the reality of witchcraft. The Indian natives had their beliefs as well on the supernatural and so did the Africans initially brought over as slaves. The Africans in particular had strong traditions about voodoo and magic. Much later, other immigrants, including but not limited to the Irish, Greeks, and Germans would also bring their old world concepts about religion and witchcraft over with them.

The first settlers, who came directly from England[13], landed on an island in the Chesapeake Bay in 1634, which they named St. Clement's Island.[14] They shortly thereafter built St. Mary's City, in southern Maryland, which was the capital until 1695 when it was moved to Annapolis.[15] The new government established a policy of relative tolerance for different Christian sects.[16] While Catholics and Protestants were butchering each other in Europe over their religious differences, people from different religious traditions managed to live in relative peace in this small province.

Founded by a Catholic Englishman, Maryland was designed as a non-exclusive sanctuary for English Catholics.[17] George Calvert had served as a Secretary of State under James I, resigned from this position after announcing that he was a Roman Catholic, which was discouraged by English law. However, he was afterwards rewarded by the king for his service by being named the first Lord Baltimore, thus making him a member of the Irish House of Lords.[18] George Calvert later sought permission from the then reigning monarch, Charles I, to settle the area that would later become the State in Maryland. Shortly after George's death, the Charter was granted to his son, the second Lord Baltimore, Cecilius Calvert, in 1632.[19]

Charles may have been sympathetic to the idea of tolerance for Catholics, as his wife was one. Perhaps her quiet advocacy played a role in the naming of the colony. Maryland, which despite what many people may think, was not named after the Virgin Mary, but instead was named after Charles I's wife, Henrietta Maria.[20] Maryland's initial charter made no explicit mention of sectarian issues, but had something of a religious theme. For example, it mentioned that the taking of the land from the original inhabitants would be justified by the belief that the "savages" who lived there had "no knowledge of the Divine Being."[21]

The charter stated there was broad authority to make laws in the province, so long as they were "consonant to Reason" and "not repugnant or contrary, but (so far as conveniently may be) agreeable to the Laws, Statutes, Customs, and Rights of this Our Kingdom of England."[22] There was no particular expression of religious tolerance in the charter, but as the province was founded by a Catholic who was suffering under English law, and he was given broad authority, with the "Advice, Assent, and Approbation of the Free-Men"[23] to make laws, so toleration of Catholics and Anglicans would have been assumed.

Religious tolerance was later established in law, in 1649, with the Act Concerning Religion. Although it granted religious toleration to Christian sects, it prohibited denying the Holy Trinity and punished this so-called crime with death.[24] However, there is no record of anyone being executed in Maryland under this law.[25]

The account of Father Andrew White, S.J. (Society of Jesus or Jesuit), a Catholic priest who sailed with the original settlers to Maryland, indicated his belief in the power of witches.[26] Writing in his "A Brieffe Relation of the Voyage Unto Maryland" Father White blamed witchcraft for some difficulties. He wrote "[a]ll next day beinge the blessed apostle St. Andrewes day, the like cloude gathered in fearefull manner, terrible to the beholders, so that ere it began to blow it seemed all the sprightes and witches of Mayland were now set in battaile array against us."[27]

It seems likely that Father White believed that the Indian tribes of the area had witches who were conspiring against them. Father White was most likely very serious in blaming witches and his opinion was not unusual for the time. There was no great understanding then of weather patterns. Most sailors were extremely superstitious and it would have been controversial for a cleric of any Christian religion not to have believed in the power of witchcraft.

Maryland was a province under the proprietary rule of the Lord Baltimore, but the charter of Maryland required him to govern with the advice and assent of the free men. An Assembly was created in 1635, although records from it were later lost. The earliest surviving records from the Assembly are from 1638.[28] In that year the following law was passed (this author's emphasis):

An Act for felonies

Be it Enacted by the Lord Proprietarie of this Province of and with the advice and approbation of the freedman of the same that these offences following in this act shall be adjudged to be felonies within this Province that is to say homiside Bloodshed committed by assault upon the pson of the Leiutenant Generall or to shed the blood of any Judge sitting in the Court Burglary, Robbery Polygamie Sacriledge **Sorcery** Petit treason Sodomy and Rape alsoe it Shall be adjudged felonie within this Province to commit Idolatry which is worshiping a false God or to commit blasphemy which is acursing or wicked speaking of God or to commit perjury which is false witness against an others life or to give or deliver to any Indian or any other declared or professed enemie of the Province any gunne pistol powder or shott without the knowledge or lycence of the Leiutenant General or to teach any other Indian or other declared enemie of the province the use of the said armes or the making thereof[29]

The narrative that Maryland was substantially more liberal than New England, where the conservative Puritans held power, is not completely accurate. Harsh laws against religious "crimes" were in place. Compared to other places in the world there was great freedom of religion in early Maryland, but only within the Christian faith.

The punishment for felonies was, unless commuted by the governor, death. For most offenses this was achieved by hanging, but the 1638/9 act also stated that (my emphasis) "[p]rovided that in offences which are petit Treason the punishment of death shall be inflicted by drawing and hanging of a man by burning of a woman **and that in the offences of sorcery and blasphemy and Idolatry the punishment of death shall be inflicted by burning.**"[30]

There is no record of any convicted sorcerer or witch being burned to death in Maryland and, as we shall see below, the law was changed.

A later act passed in 1642, distinguished between greater capital offenses and lesser ones. Treason, acts against the Lord Proprietar and making war against the province were considered greater capital offenses where the convicted would not only be executed, but his heirs would be disinherited. Lesser capital offenses of "homicide pyracy robbery Burglary Sacriledge Sodomy **Sorcery** rape polegamy and larcerny"[31] were to be dealt with by the judge "as neer as may be to the Laws of England…"[32]

It further stated that; the offendor (whether principall or accessary afore that offence committed) in any of these shall or may be Judged to suffer paines of death **or** of burning in the hand or losse of member or to lose all his or her Lands for life goods or Chattells dignity or Office or may be out Lawed exiled imprisoned dureing Life or adjudged to Serve the Lord Proprietary and his assignes for the terme of 7 or lesse years (except he be a Gentleman) or may be otherwise Corporally Corrected or put to Shame **as the Court shall think the Crime to deserve.**[33]

This slightly later law allows judges to have more leeway in the sentencing of felonies. It also does not specify the punishment of burning to death for sorcery and as the laws of England would have applied death by hanging.[34] It seems as though that would be the intention here as well.

With the basic knowledge of witchcraft laws in the 17th century, it is possible to go forward to see how individual cases involving witchcraft allegations were dealt with during this period. The early laws and history are useful in knowing how witchcraft continued to affect the culture of the Chesapeake long after witchcraft ceased to be a capital offense.

Chapter 2
17ᵗʰ Century Witches at Sea

As mentioned above, Father Andrew White believed that witches were responsible for bad weather during his journey to Maryland. James Grant in his landmark book *The Mysteries of All Nations* wrote about James I of Great Britain, who also believed that witches could be responsible for bad weather. James believed that witches had tried to kill him and his wife by raising up a storm when they were at sea.[35]

James was a zealot on the subject of witchcraft. Regarding witch trials under this monarch, Grant wrote that "[h]is brutish judges displayed unwonted activity in bringing men and women to an untimely end [for alleged acts of witchcraft], because they knew their zeal brought them into royal favor."[36] Countless people, mostly innocent, were horribly tortured and killed because of the insane imagination and irrational fears of the king. Although it should also be mentioned that later in his reign, James is thought to have become more skeptical of witchcraft claims and may have regretted some of his previous actions and beliefs.[37]

James was not alone in his odd beliefs and superstitions, although he had the unique power to use the force of law to persecute those who he suspected of witchcraft. Sailors were, and in many cases still are, a very superstitious lot. About some of their superstitions, Grant wrote:

> Sailors consider Sunday a favourable day for commencing a voyage. They are averse to proceed at sea if a lawyer or clergyman is on board. They think the presence of one of these gentlemen raises a tempest that puts their craft in peril. This superstition is probably founded on the biblical story of Jonah in his flight to Tarshish, when such a mighty tempest was raised as to endanger

the lives of those who manned the vessel that conveyed him from Joppa. Sailors are of the opinion that it is lucky to have women and children on board a ship. Time was when they objected to sail with a native of Finland as one of their crew, thinking that the Finns were leagued with Satan, and that if they were offended, they took their revenge by raising adverse winds and causing accidents to happen. Old sailors objected to have dogs on board, but cats were held sacred; and if all tales be true, Puss often secured favourable winds, and prevented shipwreck.[38]

One must remember that they were setting sail in the days before GPS, radar, radio, or any of the other modern devices that take much of the risk out of going to sea. Without much, except hope and luck, men went out to sea and sometimes never returned.

Superstition would have provided some comfort to sailors of the time. However, their beliefs were not always harmless especially when it came to alleged witches. In fact, between the common belief in witches in the 17th century and the superstitious nature of sailors, it should come as no surprise that the first witch "trials" to be associated with Maryland happened at sea.

In 1654, a complaint was filed after an extra-judicial killing of an alleged witch at sea. This was on-board a ship that had departed from England and was heading to Maryland. The *Proceedings of the Council of Maryland, 1648-1655* documents two complaints regarding an incident at sea on the ship *Charity* regarding an alleged witch, Mary Lee.

Henry Corbyne submitted a statement about the incident with the governor of Maryland at the time, William Stone, who was appointed by Lord Baltimore. The following deposition survives:

The Deposition of mr Henry Corbyn of LondonMercht aged about 25th years, Sworne and Examined in the Province of Maryland before the Governour & Councell there (whose Names are hereunto Subscribed) the 23th day of June Anno Domini 1654.

Saith That at Sea upon his this Deponents Voyage hither in the Ship called the Charity of London mr John Bosworth being Master and about a fortnight or three weeks before the Said Ships arrivall in this Province of Maryland, or before A Ru-mour amongst the Seamen was very frequent, that one Mary Lee then aboard the Said Ship was a witch, the Said Seamen Confidently affirming the Same upon her own deportment and discourse, and then more Earnestly then before Importuned the Said Master that a tryall might be had of her which he the Said Master, mr Bosworth refused, but resolved (as he Ex-pressed to put her ashore upon the Barmudoes) but Cross wids prvented and the Ship grew daily more Leaky almost to desparation and the Chiefe Seamen often declared their Resolution of Leaving her if an opportunity offerred it Self which aforesaid Reasons put the Maste upon a Consultation with mr Chipsham and this Deponent, and it was thought fitt, Considering our Said Condition to Satisfie the Seamen in a way of trying her according to the Usuall Custome in that kind whether She were a witch or Not and Endeavoured by way of delay to have the Commanders of other Ships aboard but Stormy weather prevented, In the Interime two of the Seamen apprehended her without order and Searched her and found Some Signall or Marke of a witch upon her, and then calling the Master mr Chipsham and this Deponent with others to See it afterwards made her fast to the Capstall betwixt decks, And in the Morning the Signall was Shrunk into her body for the Most part, And an Examination was thereupon importuned by the Seamen which this Deponent was desired to take where- upon She confessed as by her Confession appeareth, And upon that the Seamen Importuned the Said Master to put her to Death (which as it Seemed he was unwilling to doe, and went into his Cabbinn, but being more Vehemently pressed to it, he tould them they might doe what they would and went into his Cabbinn, and Sometime before they were about that Action he desired this depont to acquaint them that they Should doe no more then what they Should Justifie which they Said they would doe by laying all their hands in generall to the Execution of her, All which herein before Expressed or the Same in Effect this Depont averreth upon his oath to be true, And further Sayth not

> William Stone Sworne before us the Henry Corbyne Tho: Hatton day and year above written Job- Chandler[39]

The reluctance of the ship's master to authorize a trial or execution does not appear to be unusual, nor is it strange that he decided not to interfere. An uneducated and superstitious sailor of the day, as they almost all were, would have preferred to carry out a mutiny to a certain death in the sea at the hands of a witch. Fearing for the safety of his ship and of himself, the ship's master was prepared sit back and not act while his crew sacrificed this woman.

Another deposition given to the governor gives support to the idea that this killing was done against the master's orders and without his knowledge:

> The Deposition of ffrancis Darby Gent Aged about 39 yeares Sworne and Examined in the Province of Maryland before the Governour and Councell there whose Names are hereunto Subscribed the 23 day of June Anno Domini 1654.
> Saith That at Sea upon the Voyage hither about a fortnight or three weeks before the Arrivall of the Ship called the Charity of London in this Province of Maryland, whereof mr John Bosworth was then Master and upon the Same day that one Mary Lee was put to Death aboard the Said Ship as a witch he the Said mr Bosworth Seeing him this Deponent backward to Assist in the Examination of her asked this Depont why? and toul him that he was pplext about the busieness Seeing he did not know how he might doe it by the Law of England afterwards this deponent being present in the Round house heard the Said mr Bosworth give Order that nothing Should be done concerning the Said Mary Lee without Speaking first with him, and after She was put to Death or Executed to the best of this Deponents remembrance he Said he knew nothing of it, And this Deponent Saith that the Said Bosworth was in the inner room of the Roundhouse, he this deponent being in the next room at the time they treated about the busieness And this Depont could not perceive any thing either by word or Deed whereby he gave order for her Execution or putting to Death and after this he

Commanded they Should doe Nothing without his Order and al-
soe after the Execucon, expressed he knew not of it for that this
Deponent hearing these words (She is dead) ran out and asked
who was dead, and it was replyed the witch then this Deponent
Entred the next Room and Said they have hanged her and he the
Said Bosworth thereupon as it were Speaking with trouble in
a high Voyce replyed he knew not of it All which herein before
Expressed or the Same in Effect this De-ponent averreth upon
his oath to be true, And further Sayth not.
Sworne before us the day and
Yare above written
William Stone
Tho: Hatton
Job Chandler[40]

No one appears to have ever been brought to trial in relation to
this incident. The fact that Henry Corbyne and Francis Darby went to
the authorities afterwards indicates that they believed that this was an
illegal and unjustified killing, a murder.

At the same time, they failed to act to prevent her from being
harmed in the first place. Like the master, they were acting, or rather
not acting, out of fear. So although more respectable men on the ship,
including the master, knew what was happening was wrong, they refused to take the difficult decision to stand in the way of the violent
mob. Few would have done differently.

On a side note, it is an interesting question as to who Francis
Darby was. It was recorded that he was 39 years old at the time of the
incident. In the book *Maryland; the Land of Sanctuary*, the author wrote:

Father Francis Fitzherbert travelling as an unknown layman, was
a passenger on this ship when Mary Lee was hanged by the sailors. In the Jesuit Letter of 1654 the following allusion to this
occurrence is made. "The tempest lasted, in all, two months,
whence the opinion arose, that it was not on account of the
violence of the ship or atmosphere, but was occasioned by the
malevolence of witches.

Forthwith they seize a little old woman suspected of sorcery; and after examining her with the strictest scrutiny, guilty or not guilty, they slay her, suspected of this very heinous sin. The corpse and whatever belonged to her they cast into the sea. Needless to say, at such a time, it would have been worse than useless for the priest to have made any interference."[41]

A record in the Maryland Archives called St. Mary's City Men's career files states that Francis Fitzherbert was born in 1615, which could have made him 39 years old at the time of the journey. It also states that he arrived in Maryland in 1654, which was the same year that the *Charity* arrived. His title is listed as "gent esquire." Darby is referred to as a gentleman as well in the pleading above.[42]

This suspicion on this author's part triggered additional research which brought this author to a book titled *The Founders of Maryland* by Edward D. Neill. Published in 1876, it supports this author's theory that Fitzherbert and Darby were one in the same. Neil wrote regarding Fitzherbert "Francis Darby, Gent., aged thirty-nine years,deposed... and he was probably Father Francis Fitzherbert, as it was common for Jesuits to take another name, when on a journey."[43]

Even though Maryland was designed as a safe haven for Catholics, the ship would likely have contained many English Protestants, as many were immigrating to Maryland at the time.[44] They likely would not have taken kindly to the presence of a Jesuit priest as the Society of Jesus had been formed in direct response to the Reformation and members of the Society took, and still do take, a special oath of allegiance to the Pope.[45]

Using a different name would have been quite reasonable, although one wonders why he continued using his fake name while filing his statement with the Governor. While Governor William Stone was a Protestant, he served at the pleasure of the Catholic Lord Baltimore.[46]

Another early case regarding an extra-judicial killing of an alleged witch at sea was prosecuted in 17th century Maryland. John Washington, who was the great-grandfather of George Washington,[47] made a complaint in Maryland against a ship's owner, Edward Prescott, who was present when an alleged witch, Elizabeth Richardson, was hanged at sea on the way to Maryland.

The complaint was heard in Maryland's Provincial Court, sitting in the then capital of St. Mary's City. It was the only court in Maryland at the time that could hear capital and other serious criminal cases.[48]

The complaint was filed in 1659.

Regarding the Prescott witch case, the *Provincial Court Proceedings, 1659* records:

> Whereas John Washington of Westmerland County in Virginia hath made Complaynt agst Edward Prescott mercht, Accusing the sd Prescott of ffelony unto the Gouernor of this Prouince, Alleaging how that hee the sd Prescott hanged a Witch in his ship, as hee was outwards bownd from England hither the last yeare. Vppon wch Complaynt of the sd Washington, the Gour caused the sd Edward Prescott to bee arrested; Taking Bond for his appearance att this Prouinciall Court of 40000l Tob, Gyuing moreouer notice to the sd Washington by letter of his proceedings therein, (a Copie of wch lre, wth the sd Washingtons answere thereto are as followeth).
>
> Mr Washington
>
> Vppon yor Complaynt to mee tht Mr Prescott did in his uoyage from England hither cause a Woman to bee Executed for a Witch, I haue caused him to bee apprehended uppon suspition of ffelony, & doe intend to bind him ouer to the Prouincial Court to answere it,
>
> Where I doe allso exspect you to bee, to make good yor Charge. Hee will bee called uppon his Tryall the 4th or 5th of Octobr next, att the Court to bee held then att Patuxt, neare Mrs ffenwicks howse. Where I suppose you will not fayle to bee.

Wittnesses Examined in Virginia will bee of noe ualew here in this Case, for they must bee face to face wth the party accused, or they stand for nothing. I thought good to acquaynt you wth this, that you may not come un-prouided. This att present Sr is all from

Yor ffreind
29th Septembr
Josias ffendall.[49]

Josias Fendall was the Proprietary Governor and Lieutenant General of Maryland, meaning at that time he would have answered to Cecil Calvert, Lord Baltimore and the Proprietor of the Colony.[50] Fendall had ordered the ship's owner arrested for the murder of the alleged witch and told Washington that he would have to be present for the trial. Fendall's apparent respect for the rights of all people, including alleged witches, along with the right to confront witnesses should impress the contemporary reader.

As any lawyer who practices criminal law, especially prosecutors, will know, the biggest challenge can often be getting witnesses through the courthouse door. This was no exception. Washington wrote to the governor:

Honble Sr

Yors of this 29th instant this day I receaued. I am sorry tht my extraordinary occasions will not permitt mee to bee att the next Prouinciall Court, to bee held in Maryland the 4th of this next month, Because then god willing I intend to gett my yowng sonne baptized, All the Company & Gossips being allready inuited, Besides in this short time Wittnesses cannott be gott to come ouer. But if Mr Prescott be bownd to answere it the next Prouinciall Court after this, I shall doe what lyeth in my power to gett them ouer, Sr I shall desyre you for to acquaynt mee whither Mr Prescott be bound ouer to the next Court, & when the Court is that I may haue some time for to prouide euidence & soe I rest yor ffreind & Serut

30th of Septembr 1659.
John Washington.[51]

While Washington appears to be the only person who was willing to come forward to report this crime, one might question his dedication to justice since he decided not to show for the trial. However, in his defense, he did not receive notice of the trial until September 29, 1659, and was told to appear in court on October 4, 1659. Travel was not easy in those days and he had a rather important event planned, his child's baptism, where important guests had been invited. He was willing to make himself available, if given enough notice.

However, despite Washington's hope that the case would be held over, things did not go as planned. Prescott demanded a speedy trial and defended himself against the allegation. According to the court records:

> To wch Complaynt of John Washington the sd Edward Prescott (submitting himself e to his tryall) denyeth not, but that there was One Elizabeth Richardson hanged in his ship, as hee was outward Bownd the last yeare from England, & comming for this prouince, neare unto the Westerne Islands, by his Master & Company, (Hee hauing appoynted one John Greene for tht Voyage Master, though himselfe was both mercht & owner of the ship) But further sayth, That he wth stood the proceedings of his sd Master and Company, & protested agst them in that busines. And that thereuppon both the Master & Company were ready to mutiny. And it appearing to the Court by the Printed Custome howse Discharge & Light-howse Bills or acquittances produced & shewen by the sd Edw: Prescott taken or gyuen in John Greenes name; that the sd Greene was master for tht Voyage, & not Edward Prescott. And noe One comming to pro-sequute, The sd Prescott therefore prays that hee may bee acquitted.

> Whereuppon (standing uppon his Justificaon) Proclamaon was made by the Sheriff e in these uery words.

> O yes &c :

> Edward Prescott Prisoner at the Bar uppon suspition of ffelony stand uppon his acquittall. If any person can giue euidence against him, lett him come in, for the Prisoner otherwise will bee acquitt. And noe on[e app] earing, The Prisoner is acquitted by the Board.[52]

Despite the fact that witchcraft, or sorcery, was a capital offense, the law did not allow for the extra-judicial killing of witches. While some effort was put into the prosecution of this alleged murderer, the court did not postpone the case for the only prosecution witness to appear. The defendant was given a hearing, after demanding it, and gave a somewhat reasonable explanation that appeared to be supported by some documentation. Without anyone to contradict him, he was acquitted.

There is no known record of anyone else being held accountable for this murder. In many places today, especially cities such as Baltimore, it is not uncommon for serious crimes, such as murders, to go unpunished because the State was not able to produce its witnesses for trial. In this regard, little has changed since the 1600s.

These two accounts appear to be the only known cases involving extra-judicial killings of alleged witches at sea, but as we shall see in a later chapter, the superstition of seamen continued into at least the 18th century.

Chapter 3
Witchcraft Lawsuits in Early Maryland

Witchcraft allegations were made on land as well and in the early days of Maryland, defamation claims against the accusers often followed. The first recorded lawsuit, that we know of, is from 1654, where a man in St. Mary's County sued his neighbor because the neighbor had called his wife a witch. The court records provide the following information:

> Bartho: Herringe aged forty yeares or thereabouts Sworne Saith, That Peter Godson and Richard Manship meeting in yor Pettrs plantation, Richard Manship asked the Said Peter Godson whether he would prove his wife a Witch, Peter Godson replyed take notice what I Say, I came to your house where your wife layd two Straws and the woman in a Jesting way Said they Say I am a witch, if I am a witch they Say I have not power to Skip over these two Strawes and bid the Said Peter Godson to Skip over them and about a day after the Said Godson Said he was Lame, and thereupon would Maintaine his wife to be a witch
>
> Bartho: Herringe[53]

Bartho Herringe was offering testimony on behalf of Richard Manship and against Peter Godson, for defaming Manship's wife as a witch. Godson had gone to Manship's house and talked to Manship's wife. She was making fun of rumors that were swirling that she was a witch. As we will see later in the book, it was believed that witches could not easily jump over brooms or straw. Manship's wife put down two pieces of straw and for some reason dared Godson to jump over them. About a day later Godson experienced some type of injury or pain and blamed Manship's wife for causing it through witchcraft.

The next entry regarding this case reads as follows:

John Killy aged twenty five yeares or thereabouts Sworne Sayth. That at the house of Phillip Hide, Richard Manship Said to Peter Godson you Said you would prove my wife a Witch, Peter God-son answered Gentlemen take Notice what I Say I will prove her a witch beare Wittness you that Stand by.
John Killey[54]

Another witness gave the following evidence:

Margarett Herringe aged twenty three or thereabouts Sworne Saith, That Rich: Manship asked Peter Godson if he would prove his wife a witch, and Peter desired them that were present to take Notice what he Said your wife tooke four Strawes and Said in the Name of Jesus Come over these Strawes, and upon this your wife is a witch and I will prove her one.[55]

None of this even remotely proved that Manship's wife was a witch, but it did prove that Godson was quick to make allegations without having the facts to back them up. The court was rightly not concerned with any alleged evidence that Mrs. Manship was a witch, but rather with the fact that Peter Godson had defamed her as such.

It was dangerous business in those days to accuse someone of witchcraft. If Godson had evidence, he should have gone to the author-ities with it but all he had was slander, suspicion and superstition. His speed in making such heinous accusations only ensured that he would be held accountable by the court. An allegation may have been made that Godson's wife also participated in this defamation, but a record of this does not exist. Holding them both accountable, the court ruled:

Whereas Peter Godson and his wife had defamed Richard Man-ship's wife in Saying She was a witch and Uttered other Slander-ous Speeches agst her, which was Composed and Determined by the plft and defendant before mr Richard Preston,Soc as Peter Godson Should pay Charges of Warrants and Subpcenas in these Actions which Richard Manship desired may be Manifested in Court that the Said Peter Godson & his wife have acknowledged themselves Sorry for their Speeches & pay Charges.[56]

This incident was ended with the apology and the payment of money.

Thomas Mitchell, sometimes spelled Michel (spelling was not always consistent in those days), a farmer in Charles County,[57] brought a complaint to the Charles County Court in 1659, against a Ms. Hatch, the wife of a member of the Governor's council,[58] for spreading rumors that his wife was a witch. There is no indication in the record how this claim was resolved, but the *Proceedings of the County Court of Charles County, 1658-1666* present the following petition:

Thomas Michel desiereth, that Mr Thomas Lomax and Elisabeth Atwicks might haue thear oaths giuen them concerning the abusful reproaches offered unto his wife by Mis Hatche

Lomax Sworne & examined in open Court sayeth, that goodie Michel asking Mis Hatche how She did MiS Hatche replied that she thaught she had bewitched her face whearupon goodie Michell asked her if She wear in earnest or no, and She replied Shee was for shee enduered abundance of Miserie by the soarnes of her mouth and did verilie beleeue that shee was bewitched whearupon thear ware diners other circumstances past betweene the too parties which this deponant can not at presant call to rememberance onlie goodie michell tould her She woold Arest her to the Court about it, and Mis Hathce Replied that she thanght she durst not hut if she dnrst she woold endeauor to make it appear so or els she woold acknowledge she had wronged her in open Court & bee liable to their censnir & further this deponant at presant remembereth not

Elisabeth Atwicks sworne and examined in open Court sayeth that goodie Michel Asking Mis Hatche how she did MiS hatche replied that She thaught the sayd goodie Michel had bewitched her face whearupon the sayd goodie Michel asked Mis Hatch wheather she wear in earliest or no & the sayd MiS Hatch replied she

> did verilie thinck she the sayd Michel had bewitched her this is
> all to the best of this deponants rememberance at this time onlie
> thear ware diners other circumstances past which this deponant
> at presant cannant Remember[59]

Whatever the outcome of this suit was, it did not discourage witchcraft allegations against Thomas Mitchell's wife. Two years later, in 1661, Joan Mitchell, then a widow,[60] was still subjected to harassment. She was accused by people at her church of being a witch and brought suit against not only the people at her church, but also her minister.

Her pastor, the Revered Francis Doughtie, sometimes written Doughty, was apparently a Puritan-leaning Anglican from Virginia, who had previously accused at least one woman of being a witch.[61] Doughty's religious allegiances may not be certain. Russell, in the previously cited *Maryland: The Land of Sanctuary* referred to him as a Presbyterian and said he was likely the first pastor of the first Presbyterian Church in the Province of Maryland.[62]

How Doughtie ended up in Charles County, Maryland is not clear. He was not welcome in Virginia, which unlike Maryland, did not have the same tolerance for Christian faiths other than the established Anglican Church, especially for more troublesome clerics such as Doughty. Also, the fact that he was the brother-in-law of one of the provincial Governors, William Stone (who had also left Virginia due to religious disputes), made Maryland a logical place to go.[63]

On September 24, 1661, Joan Mitchell filed suit for defamation against four citizens of Charles County, including the minister Francis Doughtie, for falsely claiming that she was a witch.[64] Mitchell complained that a Miss Longe had accused her of bewitching her chickens.

Longe denied the claim and the Court threw the case out. The Charles County Court records show:

Joan Michell Plantiue The Plantiue Aresting the defendant in an
Long Defendant Action of defamation Prefereth her petition as
followeth

To the Worshipfull Commissioners of Charles Countie the humble petition of Joan Michell humblie sheweth Whearas Mis Longe
hath spoken words much tending to the taking away your Petitioners good name she humbly entreateth this Court that the
sayd Mis Long bee questioned what shee can lay to your petitioners Charge and if she haue nothing to tax your petitioner with
in the face of this Court shee humbly intreateth a vindication
with Charge of Court and your petitioner will pray hearupon
the defendant alleged that shee neuer had sayd any ill of her and
had nothing to tax her of Whearupon the Plantiue desiereth
that Richard Tarlin might haue his oath giuen him concerning the
premisses and his wife which was granted

Richard Tarlin aged 25 years or thearabouts sworne and examined in open Court sayeth that Mis Long did say that the hene and
Chickings she had of goodie Michell that the Chickings thearof
did die in such a strang manner that she thought sum old witch
or other had bewitched them and further sayeth not which was
also affirmed and no mor by the sayd Tarlins wife sworn in open
Court:

The Plantiue desireth that Francis Ferenla might haue his oath
giuen him which is granted:

Francis Ferenla sworne and examined in open Court sayeth that
Richard Tarlin did say that Mis Long did say that goodie michell
did giue her a hen and Chickings but shee thought shee had fore
spoake them and further sayeth not

the euidence beeing Circumspectedly inspected and the defendant deniing to haue miscalled lied the plantiue and also affirming
that shee hath nothing to accuse her of it is the opinion of the
bord that ther is no cause of Action it is thearfor ordered that
the Plantiue shooldbee nonsuited[65]

Mitchell had believed that Longe was defaming her and asked the court to either hear the case out. There was no real evidence of defamation produced to the court and Longe denied any wrong doing, thus the case was dismissed.

Joan Mitchell also filed suit against a James Walker alleging defamation, but again this allegation was again without evidence. The records show:

> Mr James Walker Defendant in an action of Defamation Prefereth her Petition as followeth

> To the worshipfull Commissioners of Charleses Countie the Petition of Joane Michell humbly sheweth That Whearas Mr James Walker hath spoken words tending to the taking away of your Petitioners good name shee humbly Intreateth this Court that the sayd Partye bee questioned what hee can lay to your Petitioners Charge and if hee haue nothing to taxe your Petitioner with in the face of this Court shee humbly treateth a vindication with Charge of Court and your Petitioner will pray

> The Defendant Deniing to haue spoken any ill of her and the plantine not beeing able to prooue anything against him It is thearfor Ordered tht the plantiue shoold bee nonsuited[66]

The case against her pastor, Francis Doughtie, and his son, were also unsuccessful, but do provide us with further information. Mitchell believed that the minister knew the identity of the culprit who was responsible for spreading the rumors about her being a witch, but the Pastor refused to divulge this information.

It is unclear why this would be a cause of action, but it appears that the suit never went anywhere regardless. Mitchell heard rumors that she was accused of causing another woman, who was also a member of that church, to have a tooth ache. Someone threw stones at her as a result of the allegation.

Regarding the case against the pastor, she swore out this statement against him in order to get him arrested so that he would face the defamation suit (the lines between civil and criminal claims were more blurred at that time):

Joan Michell Plantiue The Plantiue Aresting the Defendant in Francis Doughtie Minister an Action of Defamation Prefereth her Defendant Petition as followeth

To the Worshipfull Commissioner of Charleses Countie The humble Petition of John Michell your Poor Petioner as followeth

Whearas your Poor Petitioner is most shamfully and her good name taken away from her shee doath desire that shee may bee righted and that shee may bee searched by able woemen whether she bee such a person or no which thos persons say I am and if I bee found to bee such a one I may bee punished by law or els to bee Cleared by Proclamation and that the worshipfull bench woold tak it into ther serious Consideration how that I am Abused and my good name taken from mee without disart and I most humbly desire your worships that I may haue the law against them and I your poore petitioner shall bee bound to pray for you and yours

I desire tht Mr Francis Doughty may bring thos Persons to light that haue raysed this schandalous reports of mee for hee sayd that I salluted a woman at Church and her teeth fell a Aking as if shee had bin mad and I desired him to tell mee who had raysed this report of mee and hee woold not and so from one to an other my good name is taken away that I Cannot bee at quiet for them for it is all their delight and table talke how to doe mee a mischief beeing a poore distressed widow but my trust is in God that hee will plead my Case for mee and will neuer suffer the poor and innocent to perish by the hands of their Enemies for of a sunday as I was going to Church with too of Capt: Fendalls folks Mr Walkers man hurled stones at mee as I was going along and so hid himself again which for any thing that I know his master might set him on to Mischefe mee and hee himself wrongs mee by word and I your petitioner shal bee euer bound to pray for you

The Sheriff by Reson of the Defendants siknes Craueth in his behalf a Re ferance which is granted.[67]

The last line is a bit hard to understand, but it looks like the sheriff refused to arrest the minister on account of his sickness. The claim does underscore just how serious this woman was. She was begging the authorities to investigate her for witchcraft, even asking to be inspected for a witches' mark ("that shee may bee searched by able woemen whether she bee such a person or no"), a fabled mark or spot that did not feel pain and was said to be on the bodies of most witches.[68]

If an allegation of witchcraft had been made a group of women might be assembled to inspect the body of the accused for such a mark. Mitchell was clearly very upset by these allegations and was willing to put herself through the distress and trauma of such a personal and intimate inspection to prove that the allegations were untrue. The suit against Doughtie's son, Enoch, is somewhat amusing as the allegation of witchcraft related entirely to the fact that Enoch allegedly accused Mitchell of knowing how to swim, which was equivalent to an allegation of witchcraft in those days. Her complaint against him stated:

Joan Michell Plantiue

The Plantiue Aresting the defendant Mr Enock Doughti Defendant in an action of slander desiereth that her witnesses might haue thear oaths giuen them which was granted Mis Ane Cage sworne and examined in open Court sayeth that Mr Enock Doughtie Called unto goodie Michell and sayed goodie Michel goodie Michell are not you the woman that swom ouer unto Mr Pulses somtime in June last past and further sayeth not:

Mis Elenor Beane sworne and examined in open Court sayeth that goodie Michel was asked by Mr Enock Doughtie wheather she did not swime ouer unto Mr Pillses and further sayeth not

Hew neale sworne and examined in open Court sayeth that hee knows nothing of the aboue mentioned discours not any thing els apertainin unto the aboue specified Action and further sayeth not: no cause of action apearing unto the board it is ordered that the plantiue shoold bee nonsuited [69]

As a widow, without a husband to defend her in a male dominated society, filing defamation lawsuits, even without sufficient evidence, may have been a good tactic to prevent others from even considering making a witchcraft allegation against her. Although she was never apparently successful in a defamation lawsuit, she may have been following the old adage that the best defense is a good offense. If that was her plan, it worked because Mitchell was never prosecuted for witchcraft.

Overall, the courts in Maryland appear to have been cautious in their handling of civil and criminal complaints. This is perhaps a good testament to the wisdom of Maryland judges who would rather do nothing than risk greater harm by doing something that could be wrong.

In 1687, another action, this time in Somerset County (the southernmost county of Maryland and on its eastern shore) was brought by a Samuel Collins against a John Robbins and his wife, Catherine.

Collins, a bricklayer, hired an attorney by the name of James Sangster who filed the suit in the Somerset County Court. Collins and his attorney alleged that Robbins and his wife Catherine "most Wickedly & Malitiously At Severall times calumniated defamed & slandered [him] as specially in reporting & perswadeing severall of the good people of [Somerset County] that [his] wife is a witch."[70]

Catherine Robbins told a person named Henry Ledbury not to buy any living creature from Collins. Catherine told Ledbury that Collins's wife would bewitch the animals and that the animals would never thrive. Catherine Robbins also, it is alleged, promised Ledbury that she would take an oath to affirm that Collins's wife was in fact a witch. Catherine also told a Joseph Staton that Collins's wife was a witch and would prove it to him.[71]

Collins's attorney went on to state that Catherine had "induced Severall of the inhabitants of this province to creditt and believe her Slanders whereby [his] wifes life may be endangered & Comerce and dealing taken away." He alleged to have already suffered about 200 pounds sterling in damages.[72]

Evidence was heard from witnesses by the court. John Robbins had an attorney by the name of Thomas Poole who said that Robbins "never did Slander [Collins]'s wife as in the manner & forme declared."[73] He does not deny that his Mrs. Robbins may have engaged in this defamation, but only that he personally did, and appeared to offer a technical defense to the charge.

The record reflects that on September 12, 1687, the court found for the plaintiff, Samuel Collins, and ordered Robbins to pay Collins 200 pounds of tobacco (which was often used as currency in early Maryland) "with cost" and also ordered Robbins and his wife to appear next year at the Court and "in the interim to be of good behaviour Towards all his lordpps good people & especially towards Samuel Collins & his wife."[74]

It is interesting to see that there was no strict legal division drawn between criminal and civil actions at that time. Despite the fact that this was a defamation case, the court essentially put the couple on probation and ordered them to report back to the court. Also, the husband was liable for the actions of his wife, just as a husband could sue on his wife's behalf. The fact that the court wouldn't tolerate these allegations is also of note. The judges were not interested in starting a witch hunt, but rather in stopping one before it could start. An allegation of witchcraft was not only damaging to Mr. Collins's ability to earn a living, but also, potentially, to his wife's life and the public peace.

In 1702 another case involving witchcraft found its way in to a Maryland court. This complaint was also brought to a county court, not the Provincial court, so there was no possibility that capital punishment nor any serious penalty could have been inflicted on the accused.

Francis Neal Parke in his 1936 article titled "Witchcraft in Maryland" for the Maryland Historical Magazine documented this incident.[75]

According to Parke, on January 15, 1702, Charles Killburn appeared before the Anne Arundel County Court and complained that he was a victim of witchcraft practiced by a Katherine Prout. He said he was "in a very languishing condition" due to her work in the dark arts. During his illness he would sometimes recover, but then always run into Prout who was abusive and threatening toward him. Whenever he ran across her, she would wish him ill and tell him that she hoped that he would continue to suffer and die. Killburn asked the Court to investigate Prout and perhaps bring her to trial for witchcraft.[76]

The Court considered his request and demanded that Prout appear to explain herself. When she appeared she showed little respect for the Court and as a result she was fined 100 pounds of tobacco "for her misbehaviour in her Saucy Language."[77]

Nevertheless, they dismissed Killburn's petition after the Court further investigated the claim and heard evidence in open court.[78] Despite her bad behavior, the Court was not willing to jump to the conclusion that she was a witch.

The legal "saga" did not end there however, as Killburn sued Prout two months later for slander after she had called him "a rogue" and also a "foresworn rogue", which according to Parke meant that she had accused him of perjury (presumably in his complaint against her in suggesting that she may have been a witch). Killborn (or Kilburne—spelling again not always being consistent in those days) won what Parke called "a nominal victory" with damages of 6 pence. Killborn had to pay 1101 pounds of tobacco, in court costs.[79]

Later Prout would sue another woman named Kate Quillen for defamation. Quiillen had called Prout a "Dame Ye", as opposed to a "Ye Dame", which again according to Parke, meant that Quillen was calling Prout a witch as "[t]he inversion of the words carried the imputation of witchcraft, since its devotees did or said nothing in the natural order." Quillen had also accused Prout of stealing molasses and fish from a cellar in Annapolis. Prout won her suit and recovered damages of three pounds.[80]

Parke noted that there might have been other similar civil cases in early Maryland, but he did not have access to the county court records of other counties.[81] This author's review of the Somerset County records did find the story printed above regarding the defamation suit between Collins and Robbins, but has not been able to uncover anything else, although more cases from this period may very well exist. There must have been countless other allegations, especially among the servant and slave population (where such superstitions were rife) that did not make it into any court or record. It is not likely that any such records would produce an account of any actual criminal trial for witchcraft as that would have been conducted in the Maryland's Provincial Court, not a county one.

The records of the cases from the county courts that have been found show that the judges were generally much more concerned with stopping false allegations of witchcraft, which could have had violent consequences, than in actually preventing and deterring the acts of witchcraft or seeing it as a serious threat to the proprietorship. This is in contrast to the authorities in Massachusetts who rounded up and jailed over one hundred people; executing twenty of them, during the Salem witch trial episode and in even greater contrast to the witch trials in European countries such as England, France and Germany. Marylanders can take some pride in the caution and concern exercised by many of their early judicial and executive officials.

Chapter 4

17th Century and Early 18th Century Criminal Witch Trials

In Maryland witchcraft was a felony in the 17th century and the early 18th century and there were cases brought against suspected witches. Before delving in to those cases, it is first helpful to look more closely at the law and legal standards of the day in regards to witchcraft. As previously mentioned, *Country Justice* by Michael Dalton was an important book published in England in the early 17th century. It was a guide to English law for Justices of the Peace and other officials.

Referenced above in Chapter 1, to show an outline of the legal establishment's view of witchcraft, it also provided information on the investigation and prosecution of suspected witches. We know that this book made its way to Maryland and was likely consulted by at least some of the authorities.[82]

A 1690 edition is preserved on the Maryland Archive's website. There is no reason to think that earlier editions differed substantially, if at all, in regards to the subject of witchcraft.[83] In regards to witches it advised:

> Now against these Witches (being the most cruel, revengeful and bloody of all the rest) the Justices of Peace may not always expect direct Evidence, seeing all their works are the works of darkness, and no Witnesses present with them to accuse them; and therefore the better discovery, I thought good here to insert certain Observations, partly out of the Book of Discovery of the

Witches that were arraigned at Lancaster, Anno 1612. before Sir James Altham, and Sir Ed. Bromley, Judges of Assize there, and partly out of Mr. Bernards Guide to Grand-jury-men.[84]

Under English law the testimony of two witnesses to the act or a free confession with some other evidence was generally required for a felony conviction, but there appeared to be some thought given to the idea that circumstantial evidence, if compelling, might be sufficient in witchcraft cases as acts of witchcraft were generally done in private.[85]

Dalton was writing for Justices of the Peace who would not decide whether or not a person was guilty of witchcraft, since they did not decide felony matters, but rather they would consider if there was enough evidence to hold an alleged witch over for trial. Not every circumstance of guilt would be sufficient to convict, but would be enough to justify further investigation. Regarding these circumstances, Dalton advised:

1. These Witches have ordinarily a Familiar or Spirit, which appeareth to them sometimes in one shape, sometimes in another; as in the shape of a Man, Woman, Boy, Dog, Cat, Foal, Hare, Rate, Toad, &c. And to these their Spirits they give names, and they meet together to christen them (as they speak.) Ber. 107. 113. Chap. 160.

2. Their said Familiar hath some big or little Teat upon their body, and in some secret place, where he sucketh them. And besides their sucking, the Devil leaveth other marks upon their body, sometimes like a blew spot or red spot, like a flea-biting, sometimes the flesh sunk in and hollow, (all which for a time may be covered, yea taken away, but will come again to their old form.) And these the Devils marks be insensible, and being pricked will not bleed, and be often in their secretest parts, and therefore require diligent and careful search. Ber. 112. 219.

These first two are main points to discover and convict these Witches; for they prove fully that those Witches have a Familiar, and made a League with the Devil, Ber. 60.

So likewise if the suspected be proved to have been heard to call upon their Spirits, or to talk to them or of them, or have offered them to others. So if they have been seen with their Spirit, or seen to feed some thing secretly; these are proofs they have a Familiar, &c.[86]

Making any pact with the Devil was punishable by death under the Witchcraft Act of 1604, even if no harm was caused as a result. Dalton argued that these first two points regarding the alleged familiars and marks "prove fully" that the person is guilty of making an alliance with the devil. This author is not aware of any case where a person was convicted on the basis of this type of evidence alone. It would have made any person with a tick bite susceptible to a witchcraft conviction. One would think and hope that more would be required by a judge and jury.

Dalton went on to advise regarding other pieces of evidence that would be useful:

3. They have often Pictures of Clay or Wax (like a Man, &c. made of such as they would bewitch) found in their House, or which they roast, or bury in the Earth, that as the Picture consumes, so may the parties bewitched consume.

4. Other presumptions against these Witches; as, if they be given to usual Cursing and bitter Imprecations, and withal use Threatnings to be revenged, and their Imprecations or some other mischief presently followeth, Ber. 61. 205.[87]

The use of images was a popular way to practice witchcraft and still continues to be so. The fear of having one's soul stolen by a photographer continues to be a superstition among the most primitive tribesmen today. The idea that a witch could affect a person, at a distance, by the mere damaging of his form was accepted both by most of the elites of the 17th century and by those ignorant people who believed that they were in fact hurting others and practicing a dark art by the manipulation of a crude clay picture. The finding of this evidence or the testimony regarding curses, which were also believed to be effective in harming others, would have been more direct and reliable evidence in a court.

Dalton went onto state regarding witches that:

5.   Their implicite Confession: as, when any Man shall accuse them for hurting them or their Cattel, if they shall answer, You should have let me alone then; or, I have not hurt you as yet: These and the like speeches are in manner of a Confession of their power of hurting, Ber. 206.[88]

Those of us who are sometimes misunderstood or have our comments taken out of proper context could certainly appreciate the risks involved with this presumption. But words had more meaning to people in the 17th century and better judgment had to be exercised, much more than what is exercised now, by those who spoke.

Dalton continued regarding evidence against witches by writing:

6.   Their diligent Enquiry after the sick Party, or coming to visit him or her unsent for; but especially being forbidden the House.

7.   Their Apparition to the sick Party in his Fits.

8.   The sick Party in his Fits naming the Parties suspected, and where they be or have been, or what they do, if truly.

9.   The common report of their Neighbours, especially if the Party suspected be of Kin, or Servant to, or Familiar with a convicted Witch.

10.   The Testimony of other Witches, confessing their own Witchcrafts, and witnessing against the suspected, that they have Spirits or Marks; that they have been at their Meetings; that they have told them what harm they have done, &c. Ber. 212, 233.

11.   If the dead Body bleed upon the Witches touching it.

12.   The Testimony of the person hurt, upon his death.

13.   The Examination and Confession of the Children (able and fit to answer) or Servants of the Witch, especially concerning the first six Observations: sc. If the party suspected have a Familiar, or any Teat, or Pictures; her Threatnings and Cursings of the sick Party; her Enquiry after the sick Party; her boasting or rejoycing at the sick Parties Trouble: Also whether they have seen her call upon, speak to, or feed any Spirit, or such like; or have heard her foretel of this mishap, or speak of her power to hurt, or of her Transportation to this or that place, &c.[89]

The testimony of other witches alone, without more, was generally not considered sufficient, by itself, to convict. This was typically called "the devil's evidence" as the only persons offering evidence against the accused had confessed to being in league with the devil. Since the devil was "the Father of Lies" his testimony could not condemn anyone.[90] Even today the testimony of a co-conspirator alone, without more, rightly may not result in a conviction in a Maryland court.

The appearance of an alleged witch's spirit alone should not have been enough to secure a conviction.[91] It was argued that the devil could use the image of an innocent person.[92] Nevertheless, all would have agreed that this would have created a suspicion of witchcraft that would justify further investigation.

Dalton continued by writing:

14.   Their own voluntary Confession, (which exceeds all other Evidence) sc. of the hurt they have done, or of the giving of their Souls to the Devil, and of the Spirits which they have, how many, how they call them, and how they came by them.[93]

A full and open confession, in open court, would have been seen as the best evidence. But even confession alone was not sufficient. In 1646, the English Puritan minister, the Reverend John Gaule warned that "*Confession* without *Fact* may be a meer De'lusion, and *Fact* without *Confession* may be a meer 'Accident.'"[94] A free confession, with some other evidence, no matter how slight, was sufficient evidence for a conviction. And sometimes in English courts the confessions were freely given. Some may have even proud of their use of witchcraft and not afraid to die for their religion.[95] Torture or enhanced interrogation (as some prefer to call it) was illegal and rarely used and not officially tolerated in the English judicial system.[96]

Dalton also advised that:

15. Besides, upon the Apprehension of any suspected, to search also their Houses diligently for Pictures of Clay or Wax, &c. Hair cut, Bones, Powders, Books of Witchcraft, Charms, and for Pots or Places where their Spirits may be kept, the smell of which place will stink detestably.[97]

Physical evidence would always be compelling. As for the smell, judges and jurors would have had to have trusted the noses of the law enforcement officials, just as they today pretend that cops and police dogs have reliable senses when it comes to detecting the odor of marijuana and other currently illegal substances.

In order to prove that a person was engaging in witchcraft, it was helpful to be able to demonstrate that someone had been bewitched.

Dalton wrote:

Now to shew you farther, some signs to know, whether the sick party be bewitched.

1. When a healthful Body shall be suddenly taken, &c. without probable reason, or natural cause appearing, &c. Ber. 169.

2.   When two or more are taken in the like strange fits in many things.

3.   When the afflicted party in his fits doth tell truly many things, what the Witch, or other Parties absent, are doing or saying, and the like.

4.   When the parties shall do many things strangely, or speak many things to purpose, and yet out of their fits know not anything thereof.

5.   When there is a strength supernatural, as that a strong Man or two shall not be able to keep down a Child, or weak Person, upon a Bed.

6.   When the party doth vomit up crooked Pins, Needles, Nails, Coals, Lead, Straw, Hair or the like.

7.   When the party shall see visible some Apparition, and shortly after some mischief shall befal him, Ber. 173.

'But withal observe, with Mr. Bernard cap. 2. that divers strange diseases' may happen only from Natural Causes, where he sheweth eight such' several diseases, therefore, unless the Compact with the Devil be proved' or evinced by evident Marks or Tokens as abovesaid, it is not to be supposed ' that the Devil is the Agent.[98]

The English and American authorities were not insane. While accepting the belief that there were witches and that they had the power to harm others, they were conscious of the idea that the natural world had its own ability to harm people and agreed that one should not jump to the conclusion that a witch was responsible.

Living in the new world, in places such as Maryland, the early settlers were exposed to all sorts of new conditions and diseases. Ticks and other creatures would often infect people with diseases that had been previously unknown. Yet, witchcraft trials and convictions were rare in Maryland, so it is likely that most conditions were explained away as being caused naturally.

Despite this there were some accusations that made it into court and in his last part of his section on witchcraft, Dalton advised on how to properly charge suspected witches. Dalton wrote:

> And note, for the better riddance of these Witches, being duly proved to be such, there must good care be had as well in their Examinations taken by the Justices: as also in the drawing of their Indictments, that the same be both of them set down directly in the material points, &c.
>
> As, Indictments.
>
> That the Witch (or Party suspected) hath used Invocation of some Spirit.
>
> Or, That they have consulted or convenanted with their Spirit.
>
> Or, That they have imployed their Spirit, &c.
>
> Or, That they have fed or rewarded their Spirit.
>
> Or, That they have killed or lamed, &c. Some Person, &c.
>
> And not to indict them generally for being Witches, &c.
> The difference between Conjuration, Witchcraft and Inchantment, &c. is this, scil. Conjurers and Witches have person conference with the Devil, or evil Spirit, to effect their purposes.
>
> See I Sam. 28.7 &c. The Conjurers believe by certain terrible words that they can raise the Devil, and make him to tremble; and by impailing themselves in a Circle, (which, as one saith, cannot keep out a Mouse) they believe that they are therein insconsed, and safe from the Devil, whom they are about to raise; and having raised the Devil, they seem by Prayers and Invocation of Gods powerful Names, to compel the Devil to say or do what the Conjurer commands him.

The Witch dealeth rather by a friendly and voluntary Conference or Agreement between him (or her) and the Devil or Familiar, to have his or her turn served; and in lieu thereof, the Witch giveth (or offereth) his or her Soul, Blood or other Gift unto the Devil.

Also the Conjurer compacts for curiosity to know Secrets or work Miracles; and the Witch of meer malice, to do mischief, and to be revenged.

The Inchanter, Charmer, or Sorcerer, these have no Personal Conference with the Devil, but (without any Apparition) work and perform things (seemingly at the least) by certain Superstitious and Ceremonial Forms of words (called Charms) by them pronounced; or by Medicines, Herbs, or other things applied, above the course of Nature, and by the Devils help, and Covenants made with him.

Of this last sort likewise are Sooth-sayers or Wizards, which divine and foretel things to come by the flying, singing or feeding of Birds, and unto such Questions as be demanded of them, they do answer by the Devil, (or by his help) scil. they do either answer by Voice, or else do set before their eyes in Glasses, Crystal Stones, or Rings, the Pictures or Images of the Person or things sought for.[99]

The advice "not to indict them generally" expressed the English view that a person had a right to know what exactly he was charged with. Since there were so many different ways one could interact with the Devil, one had to know what one was being charged with in order to properly defend oneself. The specificity of charging was also critical to avoid the accused being acquitted on a technicality.

A conjurer could escape conviction if wrongly charged as a witch and vice versa. Despite the fact that both crimes were similar in nature and carried the death penalty, they were different offenses and had to be charged as such.

William H Cooke

Assessing how the authorities at the time had looked at the investigation and prosecution of witchcraft cases provides some insight into their thought processes as they dealt with the few witchcraft trials in early Maryland. There were only a few criminal witchcraft cases or witch hunts in early Maryland, at least compared to the rest of the world in the same time period. One can only speculate as to why Maryland never had an outbreak of mass witch hysteria while other English speaking areas in the 17th century did.[100]

Unlike colonial New England, Maryland did not have any strong democratic traditions. The proprietor owned all the land initially and appointed a powerful governor to stand in his place.[101] There was a legislative assembly, but the upper house was in the control of the governor.[102] In religious life there was no established church, but there would have been a heavier presence of Catholics, along with many Anglicans.[103] Witchcraft prosecutions often worked from the ground up and were popular with the masses. In Salem, for example, the witch trials were supported by the majority of the people, but were looked upon with skepticism by the elites, including many religious ministers.[104]

The common people in Maryland were in many ways powerless to challenge the ruling elite,[105] there was little incentive for demagogues to play on the superstitions and fears of the masses.

The fact that Maryland was a more religiously tolerant also may have played a role. While crimes such as blasphemy were on the statute books, people were free to pursue the Christian faith in any way that they pleased. Jews and others were also left alone, provided they did not insult Christianity. Because Marylanders had more of a live-and-let-live attitude toward spiritual matters they may have been less inclined to look around every corner for a witch.

Nevertheless, witchcraft was still illegal, a felony under the law and punishable by way of death, as it was in England, and sometimes cases would come to the attention of the authorities.

40

The earliest attempt to prosecute a witch within the borders of Maryland seems to have taken place on October 11, 1665, where the records of the Provincial Court state that Elizabeth Bennett was charged by the Grand Jury with practicing witchcraft, but that the indictment was not presented.[106] This might indicate that an allegation had been made, but the Attorney General, William Calvert[107], refused to ask for an indictment or one was not granted by the grand jury. Later she was cleared by proclamation.[108]

Little is known about Elizabeth Bennett or why she was charged with practicing the dark arts. However, the fact that the Attorney General was apparently unwilling or unable to gain an indictment and that she was later cleared by proclamation, should serve as sufficient evidence of her innocence, if any was needed.

The next known case of a witchcraft prosecution in Maryland involved a man, John Cowman, who was convicted and sentenced to death for sorcery around 1674. The main record that we have of him is from the Lower House of the Provincial Assembly where a petition for clemency originated.

The petition read as follows:

To the Honourable Charles Calvert Esqr Lieutenant General and Chief Iudge of the Provincial Court of the Right honourable the Lord Proprietary—

The humble Petition of the Deputies and Delegates of the Lower House of Assembly

Humbly Sheweth to your Excellency

That whereas Iohn Cowman being Arraigned Convicted and Condemned upon the statute of the first of King Iames of England &c. for Witchcraft Conjuration Sorcery or Enchantment used upon the Body of Elizabeth Goodale and now Lying under that Condemnation, and hath humbly Implored and Beseeched Us

41

your Lordships Petitioners to Mediate and Interceede in his behalf with Your Excellency for a Reprieve and Stay of Execution—

Your Excellencies Petitioners do therefore accordingly in all
Humble Manner beseech your Excellency that the Rigour and
Severity of the Law to which the said Condemned Malefactor
hath Miserably Exposed himself may be Remitted and Relaxed
by the Exercise of your Excellencys Mercy & Clemencie upon so
wretched and Miserable an Object

And your Petitioners as in Duty bound will pray &c

Signed by Order of the house Robert Ridgley Cl[109]

One may wonder why John Cowman's request for clemency gen-
erated any support within the Maryland's lower house. The answer is
not clear to history, but their advocacy on his behalf certainly benefit-
ed him. The Upper House of the Assembly, which was the governor's
handpicked council, responded as follows:

The Lieutenant General hath Considered of the Petition here
above and is willing upon the request of the Lower house that
the Condemned Malefactor be reprieved and Execution Stayed,
Provided that the Sheriff of St Maries County carry him to the
Gallows, and that the rope being about his neck it be there made
known to him how much he is Beholding to the Lower house
of Assemblie for Mediating and Interceeding in his Behalf with
the Lieut General and that he remain at the City of St Maries to
be Employed in Such Service as the Governor and Council shall
think fitt during the Pleasure of the Governor.[110]

The scene must have been a dramatic one, even if Cowman had
been told about the reprieve ahead of his mock execution. It is not
known how long he was forced to be a servant, but certainly he must
have found that a more preferable outcome.

The following two cases of witchcraft prosecutions both took
place in the 1680s and both involved women from an area that was

then Calvert County, but what would later become part of Prince George's County after it was created in 1696.[111]

The records of the Provincial Court between 1682 and 1702 are available for inspection at the Maryland State Archives in Annapolis, but these particular records have not until now been available online. This author visited the Archives and reviewed this book, which contains sometimes difficult-to-read handwritten notes of what happened at this court during this period. The records themselves were preserved, somewhat, and then later bound up in book form.

This author paid a fee to have the entire book scanned. It is available for review at the website for my book about the Salem witch trials at: http://justiceatsalem.com/earlymdcourtrecords.pdf [112]

Of course, no claims are made to any rights in this resource and it is republished as a public service. This source appears to provide the only records regarding the two above mentioned witchcraft trials in the 1680s.

Francis Neal Parke, the author of the 1936 *Maryland Historical Magazine* article "Witchcraft in Maryland" was also familiar with this source and transcribed parts of the proceedings in his article. That transcription has been used as a guide by this author, although some parts of it were not transcribed by Parke. The reader is encouraged to read the original source to check for accuracy as my recording of the old and difficult to read writing may not be perfect.

An entry states that on September 30, 1685 "The Sheriff of Calvert County further offers in open court to the Sheriff for St Marie County, the body of Richard Baulor, John Edwards, Rebecca Fowler, and Joseph Cumblinton."[113] Rebecca Fowler is the person that we are concerned with. A later entry gives the indictment, for which this author goes to Parke's work for assistance:

> The Jurors for the Rt. Honoble Lord propty of this province upon their oaths doe present Rebecca Fowler, the wife of John Fowler, late of Calvert County, planter,otherwise called Rebecca Fowler,

late of Calvert County, spinster, for that she the said Rebecca Fowler, the last day of August in the yeare of our Lord 1685 and at divers other dayes & times as well before & after having not the feare of God before her eyes but being led by the instigation of the Divell certaine evil & dyabolicall artes called witchcrafts, inchantments charms, & sorceryes then wickedly, divelishly and feloniously at Mount Calvert Hundred & severall other places in Calvert County aforesaid of her malice forethought feloniously did use practice & exercise in upon 7 against on Francis Sandsbury & several others as aforesaid last day of August in the yeare aforesaid 7 severall other dayes & times as well before as after at Mount Calvert hundred and several other places in the said County in his & their bodyes were very much the worse, consumed, pined & lamed against the peace & ct. (etcetera) and against the forme of the statute in this case made and provided.[114]

The case proceeded to trial and Fowler was tried by jury. The record reflects the result, which I am again taking from Parke after confirming its accuracy:

Upon her Endictment arraigned and upon her arraignment pleaded not guilty and for her tryall put herself upon God & Country, & Attorny Generall also. Command was therefore given to the Sheriff of St. Maries County that he cause to come here twelve. & ct.

Now here at this day to-witt the second day of October Annoq Dni 1685 came the said Thomas Burford, Attorney General for the said Lord propty and the said Rebecca Fowler was brought to the Barr and the jorors empannelled being called likewise come to-witt Randolph Brandt & Charles Egerton, James Yore, Michaell Miller, Mathew Lewis, Edward Turner, John Taunt, Andrew Insley, Justinian Tennison, James Neale, Andrew Abbington & Abraham Rhoades, who being elected, tried and sworne to say the truth in the premises doe say and deliver in writing to the Court the verdict following vizt. We find that Rebecca Fowler is guilty of the matters of fact charged in the indictment against her and if the Court find the matters contayned in the Endictment make her Guilty of witchcraft, charmes and sorceries &ct. then they find her guilty. And if the Court find those matters contained in the indictment doe not make her guilty of witchcraft, charmes sorceries & ct then they find her not guilty whereupon judgmt is respited until the Court further advices themselves upon the premises. Afterwards, to-witt the Third day of October, 1685, aforesaid came againe the said Attorney Generall for the said Lord Propty and the said Rebecca Fowler was againe brought to the barr and the Court having advised themselves of & upon the premises It is considered by the Court that the said Rebecca Fowler be hanged by the neck until she be dead which was performed the ninth day of October afores'd."[115]

Essentially what the jurors were saying was that they believed the evidence which was presented against the accused Rebecca Fowler, but left the matter to the judge as to whether or not those actions and evidence actually constituted witchcraft in the legal sense. The Court believed that it did and so Rebecca Fowler became the first known person to be killed by the authorities in Maryland for witchcraft.

The area of Mount Calvert was part of Calvert County in the 1680s, but in 1696 it became part of the then newly created Prince George's County. Mount Calvert was a city founded in 1684 and was the first town seat of Prince George's County.[116] The main section of Mount Calvert sat on the Patuxent River and today it is a park owned by Prince George's County. There is an archaeological dig there now. On a visit there recently the archaeologist in charge said that they were looking for, among other things, "witch bottles", but had not found any yet. Witch bottles, which have been occasionally found during archaeological digs, were often bottles filled with urine, seawater, earth, herbs, and various other items and were used to protect the holder from evil spells and spirits.[117] Witch bottles have been found on archaeological digs in Maryland.[118]

This author obtained and reviewed a university dissertation titled "Witches and Poisoners in Colonial Chesapeake" by Rebecca L. Logan.[119] Logan's dissertation dealt, in part, with the case of Rebecca Fowler. Logan speculated, based on her extensive research, that Fowler was Rebecca Parrot who was transported from England in 1656,[120] and then was purchased as an indentured servant by a Maryland land-owner named Henry Cox.[121] In 17th century England it was common for people, almost exclusively the poor, to be transported to America to work as indentured servants, or slaves for a period of time. This could have been as a result of a conviction for a crime; a result of her or her family going into debt; or just merely being in the wrong place at the wrong time and being kidnapped. Logan was not able to ascertain why or how Rebecca became indentured and this may be lost to history. Rebecca, Logan believed, married a John Fowler. Six men by that name were transported to Maryland during this time, but Logan assumed that the John Fowler transported by Henry Cox in 1658 was the one who married Rebecca Parrot.[122]

Despite the hardship of being indentured servants in a strange land, both were able to improve their lives. Depending on her age when she was transported, Parrot would have served a term of indenture of four or six years before she was eligible to be freed. If Rebecca had served six years from 1656 and John served four years from 1658, both may have been freed in 1662. Indentured servants were not allowed to marry, so they would have had to have been married after 1662 when both were most likely free from their indenture.[123]

While free, many challenges would still have presented themselves to this young couple. They had to work to support themselves. John took a job with a George Collins, a shoemaker, tobacco planter, and a land owner. Rebecca may have also worked for him as a domestic servant.[124] Collins was apparently fond of the Fowlers. In 1673 Collins gifted 190 acres of land to Richard Fowler, the then young son of Rebecca and John.[125] Collins also left John Fowler "one-third of the leather in his 'tann pitt'" in his will after his death in 1683. This would indicate that John Fowler also made shoes.[126]

With the money made from their work, John was able to purchase a plot of land in 1683, in an area that is now known as Prince George's County, that they called "Fowler's Delight."[127] Delightful as that piece of property may have been when purchased in 1683, neither John nor Rebecca, were destined to enjoy it for long. At the time of her trial in 1685, Rebecca was referred to within the court records as a "spinster" at the time the term may have referred to a woman who had been married but was now a widow. This could suggest that John may well have died by this point, although that is not certain.

Although at the time working for George Collins must have seemed as a blessing, with the reasonable pay and gift of land to their son, it was there that Rebecca likely first encountered one Francis Sansbury or Sandsbury, who would later be the sole named accuser against her. Sansbury was an indentured servant to George Collins and unlike the Fowlers received nothing in Collins's will when Collins died. Logan speculated that perhaps the Fowlers purchased the rest of Sansbury's indenture after Collins passed away in late 1683.[128] It was alleged that Fowler used witchcraft against Sansbury on August 31, 1685. The exact reason why Sansbury accused Rebecca Fowler of witchcraft is not known.

Logan pointed out that the indictment's use of the word "lame" as opposed to "wasted" was an indication that Sansbury may have been injured somehow.[129] This injury may have just happened after an argument with Fowler where it is possible she may have cursed him in anger.[130] Sansbury could have honestly and truly believed that Fowler was a witch, one would hope he had honest intentions or he may well have been a bitter and dishonest person who had made a false allegation for his own personal reasons.

The jurors and judges in issuing their verdict chose to believe the word of Francis Sansbury, who was at that time an indentured servant, and chose to convict Rebecca Fowler, then a land owner, of this capital offense. Their exact basis for the conviction is lost to history, but given the extreme reluctance in Maryland history to convict and execute people for witchcraft and the class advantage that Fowler would have had over Sansbury, it does not seem unreasonable to believe that the evidence may have been fairly convincing.

Logan, in her dissertation, speculated that because this trial happened during a time when the Provincial Court was engaged in other controversies and had been recently mocked by Governor Calvert, the Court may felt the need to distract the populace or reassert their authority, but Logan also conceded that this was mere speculation.[131] The full truth of the story was likely lost forever on October 9, 1685, when Fowler was hanged.

The Fowler trial did not set off a wave of witch persecutions, but another witchcraft case did come before the same court just one year later. Hannah Edwards, also of what was Calvert County, which would later be Prince George's, was indicted for witchcraft on April 29th, 1686 and brought before the Provincial Court in St. Mary's City for trial.

Using again to Parke's transcription after reviewing the primary source, the record states:

> The Jurors for the Right honble the Lord Propty of this Province, upon their Oathes doe present Hannah Edwards, the wife of Richard Edwards, late of Calvert County, Planter, otherwise Hannah Edwards of Calvert County spinster for that she the said Hannah Edwards the sixth day of February in the year of our Lord 1685 and at divers other days and times as well before and after, having not the fear of God before her eyes but being lead by the instigacon of the Devill certain evil and diabollicall arts called witchcrafts, inchantments, charmes and sorceryes, wickedly, divilishly and felloniously at Mount Calvert Hundred and several other places in Calvert County aforesaid of her malice forethrought felloniously did use practice and exercise in, upon and against Ruth Hutchinson, late of Calvert County aforesaid and severall other persons of the said County whereby the said Ruth and severall others as aforesaid the sayd sixt day of February, in the year aforesaid and several other days and times as well before as after at Mount Calvert hundred, and several other places in said County in and upon their bodyes were very much the worse consumed, pined and wasted against the peace &c and against the form of the Statute in this case made and provided &x.[132]

The date, February 6, 1685 would actually today be called February 6, 1686, as at the time in the English speaking world the new year was not observed until April 1. Regarding this case, Edwards asserted her right to a jury trial and the document reports that:

> Now here at this day to witt the Thirtyeth day of Aprill in the Eleaventh year of his Lor's Dominion &c Anno Dni 1686 came Thomas Burford, Attorney Generall aforesaid and the said Hannah Edwards sett to the Barr And the Jurors empannelled likewise came to witt Richard Smith, Andrew Abington, Walter Lane, James Neale, John Atky, Thomas Truxton, John Allin, John Woodward, Moses Jones, Robert Benson, Thomas Price and Thomas Cooke, who being thereto tryed and sworne to say the truth in the primises does say upon their oath that the said Hannah Edwards is not Guilty of the Endictment aforesaid or the witchcraft whereof she standes indicted.[133]

According to Logan, Edwards had been a widow, but was at the time remarried (which might explain why she was referred to as a "spinster" and perhaps suggests that Rebecca Fowler may have previously been married as well, if John Fowler was alive in 1685).[134] Edwards had quite a bit of hardship in her life, including the deaths of her step-children at the hands of Indians.[135] Having overcome some financial hardship, the couple was able to later purchase a home and furniture. They had also started to invest in cattle just before she was accused.[136] Little is known about Ruth Hutchinson. Logan speculated that she might have also been an indentured servant, but she had no hard evidence to support this speculation.[137]

We know little about her trial, except that she had one. Edwards was accused of causing Hutchinson to be "consumed, pined, and wasted," as opposed to Fowler who was accused of causing her victim to be "consumed, pined, and lamed."[138] As previously noted, laming usually meant that there was some sort of bodily injury, while a wasting disease could be seen as something much more of a vague accusation. Logan pointed out that Hutchinson was still alive some twenty-three years later.[139]

The jurors may not have been convinced that Hutchinson was really harmed. The jurors may have thought that Edwards was completely innocent. We do not know why Edwards was acquitted, just as we don't know why Fowler was convicted. Two of the jurors who served on Edwards's trial had also served on Fowler's trial, so the jury pool was not completely different.[140] Logan speculated that perhaps the fact that Fowler was originally an indentured servant, while Edwards's first husband was part of the gentry, may have been a reason for the different outcomes.[141] But Fowler was not an indentured servant at the time of her trial and she was convicted on the word of one. Logan suggested that Ruth Hutchinson, Edwards's alleged victim, may have appeared less than honest to the court.[142] Hutchinson later got into further trouble with the authorities for having a child out of marriage (which was a crime) and had later to indenture herself in 1704 to pay off debt, and even indentured her "sister, servant, and apprentice" in 1709 for five years to pay for medical care for her leg.[143]

Logan concluded her remarks on Hutchinson by writing:

Ruth Hutchinson is something of an enigma. She apparently didn't marry, which was unusual, and she was never given an occupations designation in the records. The 1709 indenture is especially puzzling. Why would Ruth's sister also be her servant and apprentice? Ruth was an adult, probably in her forties; presumably her sister was also an adult. Why did Ruth have the power to indenture her? Furthermore, what kind of apprentice could Ruth have? We don't have enough information to understand Ruth Hutchinson. However, there seems to have been something disreputable about her. It's possible the jurors did not believe her testimony.[144]

The search for truth often rests on the credibility of witnesses alone. Even today most criminal cases do not solely rely on forensics or video evidence, but on what a person says he or she personally witnessed. If a witness is seen as anything less than completely reliable then a defendant will usually not be convicted. The jurors in Hannah

Edward's case may have taken the wise and safe decision to acquit because the alleged victim did not seem trustworthy.

The Attorney General, who prosecuted both cases, and who secured the only capital witchcraft conviction and execution in Maryland, was Thomas Burford. He was a lawyer from Charles County who had previously served in Maryland's lower house.[145] Recorded in his possessions at the time of his death shortly thereafter in 1687 was a copy of the previously mentioned *Country Justice* by Dalton.[146] One can picture the prosecutor reviewing the book and taking notes on it to prepare for these unusual cases.

One could also reasonably conclude that the jurors in both of these cases must have taken their oaths seriously and were convinced that Fowler was guilty but were not convinced that Edwards was. Whatever the truth was, it would be difficult to argue from these facts that the justice system was fundamentally unfair.

The last known incident of a criminal prosecution for felony witchcraft in Maryland took place in 1712, which must have even struck people at the time as odd. After the Salem witch so-called hysteria died in late 1692, many people in the English speaking world, especially educated ones, started to take a dimmer view of witchcraft trials. It was accepted that many innocent people had been wrongly convicted and executed at Salem and the zeitgeist had turned against witch hunts.[147] Nevertheless, witchcraft was still a crime under English and Maryland law and prosecutions could be lawfully brought.

The capital of Maryland had moved before 1712 to its present seat in the city of Annapolis[148] and the Provincial Court, still Maryland's highest criminal court where only capital cases could be heard, moved there also. The Attorney General, then William Bladen, brought a case before the grand jury against Virtue Violl of Talbot County, on Maryland's eastern shore, for witchcraft.

Given the previously mentioned superstitions against sailing with a witch, one must wonder if her captors were apprehensive as they brought Violl across the sometimes somewhat choppy waters of the Chesapeake in what must have been a not very large sailboat. They must have taken that route, as she was brought safely to trial, and it seems unlikely that the Sheriff of Talbot County would have made the far longer journey up the eastern shore, through the then wilderness of Cecil County and then down the western shore to Annapolis simply to avoid the water. Perhaps even he doubted the allegations against Violl or merely decided to take his chances.

This author has reviewed the original court record at the Hall of Records in Annapolis and agrees with Parke that the indictment stated:

> The Jurors for our Sovereigne Lady that now is of Great Brittain &c To-witt Jno. Bozman, John Taney, Notely Maddox, Edward Veazey, Wm. Denton, Arnold Elzey, Wm. Willoughby, Wm. Stevens, James Monat, Henry Autstin, Philemon Armstrong, Ubgate Reeves, Joseph Harrison, Wm. Sweatnam, James Keech, Joshua Cecill, Paul Bussey, Tho Taylor, Patrick Dunkin, Thos. Tolly, Thomas Thackstone, Wm. Gray, Jona Back and Thos. Price, good and lawful men elected tryed and sworn to speak the truth upon their oath do present Virtue Violl of sd. County of Talbott spinster otherwise called Virtue Violl of the sd. County of Talbott spinster the nineteenth day of August in the eleventh year of the reigne of our said Lady the Queen that is now of Great Brittaine etc. At Talbot County, afd. the fear of God before her eyes haveing but being Seduced by the devil most wickedly, & diabollically did use practice & exercise witchcraft whereby & wherewith she did waste, consume and pine the body of a certaine Ellianor Moore of the afd. County spinster then & there in the peace of God and our said Lady the Qeen being with such her most wicked and Diabollicall use practice & exercise of witchcraft the Tongue of the said Elinor Moore did then and there at divers times before within the County lame & render speechless to the great displeasure of Almighty God & agst her majtys peace and the form of the statute in that case made and provided. W. Bladen Att gen who followeth for our Lady the Queen.[149]

The reader may notice a subtle difference between the style of this indictment and the previous ones as the Lord Proprietor of Maryland was not mentioned, but instead only the Monarch, in this case, Queen Anne. This is because in 1689, following the example of the Glorious Revolution in Britain and Ireland, the then majority Protestant population overthrew the Proprietary Government of the Calverts, then under the control of Charles Calvert, and Maryland became a colony with a Governor appointed by the Crown.[150]

A detailed allegation was made against Virtue Violl, which had not been seen in any previous witchcraft indictments in Maryland, in that she allegedly achieved a specific result, causing the tongue of Elinor Moore to be rendered speechless. The record reflects that the following witnesses were called: Elinor Moore [the alleged victim], Capt. Jno Needles, Mrs. Needles, Robt. Jadwin, Saml Hatton, Thoas Silvester.[151] Other than the alleged victim, it is not clear which side the other witnesses testified in support of. In the event that Moore was able to give testimony, it would certainly seem to hurt her claim that Violl had rendered her speechless. One could argue that if Violl really had this power she would have exercised it at the trial where she was facing a death sentence if convicted.

It seems likely that this was nothing more than the result of a bitter dispute between these two women. Violl may well have made some comment to Moore along the lines of wishing that her tongue would fall out, perhaps in response to some hurtful or malicious statement that Moore had made. Being overly dramatic, Moore may have believed that she was bewitched by Violl and may have had trouble speaking. Talbot County was not well connected to the rest of the educated and apparently more civilized world and thus such superstitions of witchcraft may well have continued much longer there than elsewhere in the modern world.

Regardless of what transpired at the trial, the jury rendered a verdict of not guilty on October 7, 1712.[152] The men who served on the jury might have looked at this case with a bit more sophistication and been more level-headed than these two feuding women from Maryland's eastern shore. Virtue Violl and the witnesses would have returned home, hopefully to live more peaceful lives without accusation.

One must wonder why William Bladen, the Attorney General, even prosecuted this case. Bladen, originally from Yorkshire, England came to Maryland as a Custom's officer for the port of Annapolis.[153] He became ingrained in the civic life of Annapolis, serving as, among other things, as Vestryman at St. Anne's [then Anglican, now Episcopal] Church and as a city Alderman.[154] There is no reason to think that Bladen had any particular agenda when it came to witchcraft. He is not known to have prosecuted any other witch cases. He is not known to have spoken out for or against such trials. So what went through his mind when he brought this case to trial? Was he looking simply to give the alleged victim her day in court but did not push very hard for a conviction? That seems like a reasonable possibility.

Bladen was a political figure and at least one scholar had suggested that he prosecuted cases not out of a sense of justice, but out of cynicism. C. Ashley Ellefson, in his work *William Bladen of Annapolis, 1673?-1718:"the most capable in all Respects" or "Blockhead Booby"?*, made the point that Bladen was not overly successful in gaining convictions as an Attorney General, despite the fact that criminal defendants had far fewer legal protections than they do today. Ellefson suggested that Bladen may have viewed prosecuting innocent people as just as important as prosecuting guilty ones as it sent a message to people in the community not to stand out or draw attention to themselves, lest they find themselves in the dock.[155] No one wants to be on trial, even if his chances of acquittal are good. A witchcraft prosecution might have also sent the message that he was serious about enforcing all laws, even ones that had for the most part been neglected in the past several years.

Violl was almost certainly the last person charged in Maryland with the capital offense of witchcraft. The spirit of the times was changing and in 1736, Parliament in London passed an act removing the death penalty for witchcraft. It ceased to be a felony under the law. The elites in government no longer believed in the power of witchcraft. 9 George 2 Chapter 5 read:

9 George 2, Cap. 5.—*An act to repeal the statute made in the first year of the reign of king* James *the first, intituled* an act against conjuration, witchcraft, and dealing with evil and wicked spirits *except so much thereof as repeals an act of the fifth year of the reign of queen* Elizabeth, *against conjurations, enchantments and witchcrafts, and to repeal an act passed in the parliament of* Scotland *in the ninth parliament of queen* Mary, *intituled* anentis witchcrafts, *and for punishing such persons as pretend to exercise or use any kind of witchcraft, sorcery, enchantment or conjuration.*—Be it enacted by the king's most excellent majesty, by and with the advice and consent of the lords spiritual and temporal, and commons, in this present parliament assembled, and by the authority of the same, that the statute made in the first year of the reign of king *James* the first, intituled *an act against conjuration, witchcraft, and dealing with evil and wicked spirits,* shall, from the twenty-fourth day of *June* next, be repealed and utterly void and of none effect except so much thereof as repeals the statute made in the fifth year of the reign of queen *Elizabeth,* intituled *an act against conjurations, enchantments and witchcrafts.)*

II. And be it further enacted by the authority aforesaid, that The act in from and after the said twenty-fourth day of *June,* the act passed in a Maria also the parliament of *Scotland* in the ninth parliament of queen *Mary,* repealed, intituled *anentis witchcrafts,* shall be and is hereby repealed.

III. And be it further enacted, that from and after the said twenty-fourth day of *June,* no prosecution, suit or proceeding, shall be commenced or carried on against any person or persons for prosecuted witchcraft, sorcery, enchantment or conjuration, or for charging another with any such offence, in any court whatsoever in *Great Britain.*

IV. And for the more effectual preventing and punishing any pretences to such acts or powers as are before mentioned, whereby exercise ignorant persons are frequently deluded and defrauded; be it further enacted by the authority aforesaid, that if any person shall, from and after the said twenty-fourth day of *June,* pretend to exercise or use any kind of witchcraft, sorcery, enchantment or conjuration, or undertake to tell fortunes, or pretend from his or her skill or knowledge in any occult or to discover where or in what manner any goods or chattels, supposed to have been stolen or lost, may be found; every person so offending, being thereof lawfully convicted on indictment or information in that part of *Great Britain* called *England,* or on indictment or libel in that part of *Great Britain* called *Scotland,* shall for every such offence suffer imprisonment the space of one whole year without bail or mainprize, and once in every quarter of the said year in some market town of the proper county upon the market day, there stand openly on the pillory by space of one hour, and also shall (if the court by which such judgment shall be given shall think fit) be obliged to give sureties for his or her good behaviour, in such sum, and for such time, as the said court shall judge proper according to the circumstances of the offence, and in such case shall be further imprisoned until such sureties be given.[156]

Of course, even though Maryland had its own legislature, its laws, according to its founding charter, could not be repugnant to the laws of England. One would think that felony witchcraft laws would be considered repugnant by this point. That certainly appears to be the case as there were no felony witchcraft prosecutions after 1712.

It is important to underline that *pretending* to be a witch was viewed as an offense as it could disturb the peace of a community. The penalty for this offense may seem harsh, but it was certainly much lighter than death. There is no record of a Marylander being criminally prosecuted for pretending or posing as a witch.

William Kilty, an Englishman who later immigrated to America and fought for a Maryland revolutionary regiment during the Revolutionary War and later became a Federal Judge,[157] wrote a book with an extremely long title by the name of; *A report of all such English Statutes as Existed at the Time of the First Emigration of the People of Maryland: and Which by Experience Have Been Found Applicable to their Local and Other Circumstances; and of Such Others as Have Since Been Made in England or Great-Britain, and Have Been Introduced, Used and Practised, by the Courts of Law or Equity; and also all Such Parts of the Same as may be Proper to be Introduced and Incorporated into the Body of the Statute Law of the State.*

In the book he explained all of the English laws that he could find and researched how they had been used, if at all, during Maryland's history and offered opinions over whether or not they should be adopted by the Government of post-revolutionary Maryland. Due to Maryland's unique history as a haven for Catholics and other non-Anglicans, not all of the laws of England were immediately applied in Maryland during the proprietary Government, but only those considered suitable for the province and her people were adopted. Kilty made note of the 1736 law which punished those who *pretended* to be witches and wrote that he had "met with no instance of a prosecution under the last part of this statute."[158] Kilty thought it was unnecessary to incorporate this statute into Maryland's post-revolutionary law as there were then "no persons being now found so absurd as to pretend to exercise such witchcraft."[159] As we shall see Kilty was very much mistaken.

Chapter 5
Witchcraft Legend, Lore, and Fact in the 18th and 19th Centuries

Where the official records stop, legend and folklore pick up and provide several stories of suspected witches in Maryland. Some of the stories had a basis in reality. Others may have been merely imagined or invented.

Folklore says there was a witch named Moll Dyer in St. Mary's County who may have been chased out of town in either the late 17th or early 18th century. Little historical documentation seems to exist regarding this alleged witch. In the absence of primary historical evidence and due to the fact that the story regarding her may more popular legend than fact, I feel comfortable with printing the story as told by Wikipedia Contributors. Often in folklore, what is popular becomes what is "true". Wikipedia Contributors state, in part, regarding Dyer:

> **Moll Dyer** (died c. 1697?) is the name of a legendary 17th-century resident of Leonardtown, Maryland who was said to have been accused of witchcraft and chased out of her home by the local townsfolk on a winter night. Her body was found a few days later, partially frozen to a large stone. Stories say her spirit haunts the land, looking for the men who forced her from her home. The land near her cabin is said to be cursed, never again growing good crops, and an unusual number of lightning strikes have been recorded there.[160]

William H Cooke

The Wikipedia Contributors also reported:

The story has survived for generations, though no historical record has been found of Moll Dyer's existence. Records from
the colonial period are often incomplete and the County Courthouse burned in 1831 so early documents were lost. Historical
evidence includes:

- An immigration record shows that Mary Dyer, Marg. Dyer,
  and Malligo Dyer were transported to Maryland in October 1677 on a ship commanded by Capt. Thomas Taylor (Maryland Hall of Records Land Books, Liber 15, Folio
  438). (Moll is a nickname for Mary.)

- A "great epidemic" occurred in Southern Maryland in
  1697/98. (Archives of MD, V23, p. 396)

- In the 18 August 1892 edition of *The St. Mary's Beacon* (Edi-
  tion 604, Volume LII), Joseph F. Morgan wrote that Moll
  lived in the area for many years, and that her cottage was
  burned while "Cotton Mather held sway in the land of the
  Puritans." (Mather was born in 1663 and died in 1728.)
  This story has been reprinted in the "Chronicles of St.
  Mary's," which are available from the St. Mary's County
  Historical Society.

- There were several witchcraft trials in Maryland, starting in 1654 and continuing until 1712. Rebecca Fowler of
  neighboring Calvert County was hanged as a witch on 9
  October 1685 (Maryland Historical Magazine XXXL p.
  271-298).

The *Washington Times* has called her "perhaps Maryland's best-
known bit of witch lore". Local newspapers reprint the story
from time to time.[61]

The Wikipedia Contributors also reported about a stone associated with her. They wrote:

According to legend, Moll Dyer rested on a large stone before she died, leaving indentations (either hands or knees or both) behind. In 1972, an 875-pound boulder was moved from a wooded ravine near Moll Dyer Road to the Leonardtown courthouse lawn in front of the old 1848 jailhouse, which now serves as the St. Mary's County Historical Society building, and is there to this day.[162]

Moll Dyer may have also served as inspiration for the successful 1999 movie, *The Blair Witch Project*. Whether the legend of Moll Dyer is true or not, the story continues to frighten and entertain children and adults today in St. Mary's County.

Moll Dyer was not the only legendary witch reported to inhabit Maryland. Others have made their way into the legends and traditions of the land on the Chesapeake.

One supposed witch, Sarah McDaniel, lived in Annapolis around the middle of the 18th century. We have at least one contemporary account of her.

The *Maryland Historical Magazine* in 1919 published an earlier work titled "A Notice of Some of the First Buildings with Notes of Some Early Residents" by Rebecca Key. Key was born in 1754 and her writings provide with us information about life in Annapolis at the time. She wrote the following about an incident in her youth involving Sarah McDaniel and the launching of a boat:

> The only vessel whose name I recollect was called "The Lovely Nancy" after Mrs. Roberts, an intimate acquaintance with whom I used to play in childhood. I remember the name from an incident connected with the launching. She was on the stocks and a large concourse of people assembled to see the launching. An old woman named Sarah McDaniel (white), a fortune-teller and a witch, who was standing by said "The 'Lovely Nancy' will not see water to-day." She moved finely for a while but stuck at last and Captain Slade with his sailors, fully under the impression that the vessel had been bewitched, determined to duck the old

woman. They searched for her busily two or three days during which time she lay secreted in my father's kitchen, which stood adjacent to his dwelling on the lot opposite to Mrs. Walshe's residence.[163]

Key wrote that this event happened at the shipyard which was then "[w]ithin the point of land projecting between the College and Graveyard,"[164] meaning between what is now St. John's College and St. Anne's Episcopal Church. The water then extended up farther and was deep enough to launch ships. Key wrote that the Lovely Nancy did make it into the water and "made several prosperous voyages."[165]

Another source also mentioned this incident. David Ridgely in 1841 compiled and edited *Annals of Annapolis* where he passed on this story:

Tradition tells us, that they [ship builders Kirkwell and Blackwell] built the 'brig Lovely Nancy'—at the launch of which the following incident occurred. She was on the stocks, and the day appointed to place her on her destined element, a large concourse of persons assembled to witness the launch, among whom was an old white woman named Sarah McDaniel, who professed fortune-telling, and was called 'a witch.' She was heard to remark—'the Lovely Nancy will not see water to-day.' The brig moved finely at first, and when expectation was at its height to see her glide into the water, she suddenly stopped, and could not be again moved on that day. This occurrence created much excitement amongst the spectators; and captain Slade and the sailors were so fully persuaded that she had been 'bewitched,' that they resolved to duck the old woman. In the meantime she had disappeared from the crowd; they kept up the search for two or three days, during which time she lay concealed in a house that stood on the lot opposite to the present dwelling of Robert Welch, of Ben. Esquire.

The 'Lovely Nancy' did afterwards leave the stocks, and is said to have made several prosperous voyages.[166]

Key, the primary source, was born in 1754[167] and seems to have described a scene from her youth it is likely that this incident occurred in the 1760s or 1770s, decades after witchcraft ceased to be considered a supernatural occurrence or a felony. The belief in witchcraft, magic, and superstition continued, however, especially among sailors. As noted previously, sailors were a superstitious group and many still continue to be so even to this day. For example, many still believe that whistling on-board a ship or allowing a woman to sail with the crew will bring bad luck.

Sarah McDaniel did not run to the authorities for help when chased by the captain and his crew and it appears that they feared no sanction for attempting to inflict the punishment of dunking on her, although one would think that had they killed her they would have been prosecuted. The law may well have tolerated the infliction of some private punishment on the alleged witch, but not anything resulting in death or serious bodily harm. Dunking in water could have been extremely dangerous and might have resulted in death or serious physical harm, but usually it did not and fortunately for Ms. McDaniel she found a safe place to hide in the kitchen of Ms. Key's father.

Belief in witchcraft in Maryland certainly did not die out after the Revolution. An incident from Worcester County, now home to Ocean City, Maryland, and other resort areas, reminds us that many people still believed in the power of the dark arts. The Journal of the State Council, 1784—1789, presents us with this entry from February 6, 1787 which reports:

> A Petition from Samuel Smith of Worcester County was laid before the Board setting forth, that through ignorance he was induced to believe in Witchcraft, which belief drew him into a Riot, for which he was charged before, and fined by the Court of the County aforesaid, in the Sum of Thirty pounds, for the payment of which and incident charges, he is now confined in the Gaol of said County—that he has a wife and several Children, and that having served in the Army during the late War, he is in Circumstances too low to pay the said fine. The facts set forth being countenanced by three of the Magistrates of said County, who recommend a Remission of the fine, the Board in

Consideration of the low Circumstances of the Petitioner, and the Expence and trouble he has already incurred, do order and direct that Twenty eight pounds, ten shillings of the fine be and is hereby remitted.
W. Smallwood
John Kilty
John Davidson[168]

John Kilty, who served on the State Council, which greatly reduced Smith's fine, was the brother of William Kilty,[169] mentioned above, who wrote after the Revolution that were "no persons being now found so absurd as to pretend to exercise such witchcraft." Yet, here was Mr. Smith claiming that he had become seduced by witchcraft and acted out because of it.

Taking us back to Annapolis, there is a local legend regarding a witch whose ghost is said to inhabit Truxtun Park. Truxtun Park is an area off of Spa Creek where people go to walk or run, play tennis or other sports and to launch boats. Out on the outskirts of the park, near the baseball field off of Hilltop Lane (38 57 44.03n, 76 30 07.50W on your GPS device) there is a small grave or crypt and allegedly there are more graves although they are covered by the dirt and grass.

According to the local tales, the witch of Truxtun Park was interred there years ago, possibly in the 1800s and at night she stalks the park. It is said that on some nights you can see the ghosts of her victims hanging from the trees. One legend says that the witch was hanged from one of the trees in the park and sometimes her ghost is seen hanging. Of course, there is no documentation to support this story. Mary Young Woodward Hesselius, a Methodist woman who lived on the property in the early 19th century, is thought for some reason to be the real person behind the witch legend, for reasons unknown. It is thought that the grave reported to be that of the witch may indeed belong to a businessman, Captain Louis Neth, who in the 19th century purchased the property.[170]

There does not appear to be any evidence to support the rumors and stories that a witch ever lived on the property, let alone that she was buried there and still haunts the place. Still, why let facts get in the way of a good story?

It is hard to tell how tales and legends like this get started, but they tend to take on a life of their own after a while. It has been speculated that this story was invented to keep children out of the park when it was privately owned. However, a good witch or ghost story usually has the opposite effect.

This author, who currently lives near the park, will sometimes watch out for the witch and look for the ghosts of her victims while walking home at night from the bar, although one should be far more concerned with the gang members who recently have taken to spraying their graffiti all over the park. If only the witch were real and she would appear to these gang members and scare them away.

Another local witch legend brings us back to the eastern shore, to Talbot County. This alleged witch, named Katie Coburn, lived in the area of Plaindealing Creek, which was named so because it was settled by Quakers, religious non-conformists and dissenters from the Church of England who were known for their honesty and simplicity. It was said that they "dealt plainly" or fairly with the local Indian population, which differentiated them from the other settlers. Thus 'Plaindealing Creek' was an apt name for the area and its inhabitants.

This author could not find any reported court cases involving Ms. Coburn and it cannot even be said for certain that she actually existed or if so, when exactly.

The main source of information regarding her existence was a book published in 1898, *Land of Legendary Lore: sketches of romance and reality on the eastern shore of the Chesapeake*, by Prentiss Ingraham.

According to Ingraham:

William H Cooke

[Plaindealing Creek] was the ideal spot for spooks to haunt, while to enhance the dismalness of the old abode, it became the dwelling place of an old woman known as "Katie Coburn, the Witch." This "witch," the last of her kind known in Talbot, was old, deformed, hideous, and was guilty of diabolical ways and impish incantations to make herself feared. That she was dreaded by all, especially the children and negroes, there was no doubt, for the former were kept out of mischief by being threatened with her, and the latter felt that the sight of her was a hoodoo upon them. The negroes accordingly gave Witch Katie a very wide margin of room when they met her, and wore charms to counteract her spells, the "left hind foot of a rabbit, killed at the dark of the moon," doubtless being in great demand after a meeting with the "Witch of Plaindealing."

Not far from Plaindealing there lived a farmer whose cows pastured near the old burying-ground. One afternoon the boy whose duty it was to drive the cows home had to go near the lonely spot, and beheld to his amazement a stranger there ;—a man tall, stately, in the ancient garb like that worn by those whose portraits were in the deserted mansion. The man spoke to the boy, but the latter tied for home, told his story, and it was not believed. Again he saw the same man, and again, until at last he spoke to him, and for response saw him walk to a certain spot in the burying-ground and point downward, at the same time stamping his foot. This same performance was gone through with several evenings after, between the boy and the silent spectre in quaint old time costume.

On one occasion the spectre led the boy, now no longer afraid of him, into the old home and pointed to a portrait on the wall. The boy saw that the "ghost" was strangely like the portrait, dress and all. Then he was led back to the grave yard and the spectre pointed downward and stamped his foot, as before. As it was growing dark, and the cows had gone on ahead, the boy suddenly decided to go home, and he lost no time in doing so, his parents again laughing at his story. But then came the rumor that "Witch Katie" had not only disappeared from Plaindealing, but also from the country. The boy had not seen her since the coming of the quaint man of the grave-yard.[171]

A similar but somewhat shorter version of the story was told in an 1886 edition of *McBride's Magazine.*

According to *McBride's:*

> [Plaindealing] was the very place for a first-class ghost story, and its fitness was heightened by the residence on the premises of Katie Coburn, the last witch of Talbot. This poor old creature, lonely, deformed, repulsively ugly and wretchedly poor, was a terror to negroes and children far and near, who had marvelous tales of her impish ways and diabolical cantrips.[172]

It seems reasonable to think that at least part of the legend is true. A deformed woman may have lived in the area and some, especially the young and uneducated in the 17th, 18th or 19th century, may have believed that she was a witch. Whether or not she actually was or was not a witch, or really just wanted others to think that she was, is anyone's guess. As I argued in *Justice at Salem: Re-examining the Witch Trials*, there could be certain advantages to having other people think that you were a witch. For example, others might have thought twice about harming you if they feared that you might seek revenge using your supernatural powers. For a poor defenseless woman who had no power in her society, this could well have been her only means of self-defense against other people who might have otherwise taken advantage of her.

Although if she did disappear mysteriously it may have been that foul play was involved and her body was disposed of in the creek. A drawback of having others think you are a witch is that occasionally someone may drum up the necessary (probably liquid) courage and do away with you.

This author has driven out to the area of Plaindealing to investigate. The creek seems to be surrounded by houses and private properties. There appears to be no interest in encouraging tourism to the area or of popularizing the legend of this alleged witch. Most of the people seem as though they could do without visitors stalking through the area.

Just south of Talbot County on the eastern shore is Dorchester County. There are not any recorded reports of witch trials from the county, but the area still has traditions related to the topic Published in 1902, *History of Dorchester County, Maryland* by Elias Jones detailed some of the beliefs of the locals, both white and black, regarding witchcraft under the chapter titled "Folklore and Superstitions". Jones wrote:

WITCHES
A broomstick laid across the doorway will prevent a witch from entering the house.

If a witch sits down in a chair in which is sticking or is afterwards stuck a fork, she cannot rise as long as the fork stays there. An example of this was tested at the "Dr. Johnson" place in "Lakes" with old "Suf," who was said to be a witch.

A witch can take a horse from a locked stable and ride it all night; the evidence of this being the foaming sweat on the horse and the witchknots tied in its tail and mane, often seen the next morning.

A witch can turn people into horses and ride on them. One man in Dorchester County died from the effects of such a trip, the clay being found under his finger and toe nails. He had refused to let the witch have his horse to ride, so she rode the owner instead.

If a witch is about to turn a sleeping person into a horse and the sleeper awakes in time, seizes the witch and holds her without speaking until daybreak, she will assume her proper form.

A witch can also turn herself into any animal she pleases for hunter's dogs often trail and tree witches at night that take the form of some animal to avoid detection.

To kill a witch, draw a picture of her and shoot at it with pieces of silver instead of lead, bullets or shot; just where the picture is shot the witch will be wounded; if in vital parts of the body, she will die from the effects.[173]

Many accounts of witchcraft are most likely the result of sleep paralysis, a condition which causes a person to wake while still remaining in the dream state. The person is unable to move as the body paralyzes itself during the dream state to avoid any bodily injuries. Still in the dream state, but somewhat awake, often the person sees disturbing visions, such as ghosts, aliens, or witches, but is unable to react while he imagines that things are being done to him. This could explain the stories about witches riding people at night.[174]

The last section about killing the suspected witch documents the fact that witchcraft itself was often used as a tactic to defend against witches. Image magic, attacking a representation of a person to inflict pain or death on him or her was a thought to be a common practice amongst witches and others in almost every society.

From a physiological and psychological standpoint, if one believes in the power of witchcraft and believes that a witch is practicing image magic against one, then this alone could have a dramatic and negative effect on a person's health. A person who herself practiced witchcraft would be highly susceptible to the negative effects of knowing that another person was engaging in image magic against her. The stress on the person could be enough to actually kill someone and likely did succeed in some cases when employed. The use of the same tactic to kill an alleged witch does not change the fact that the person doing it is still practicing witchcraft. The person attempting to kill a witch through shooting at her image becomes exactly what he seeks to destroy.[175]

Studies in Philology, published in 1919 by the University of North Carolina, contained an article titled "Witchcraft in North Carolina" authored by Tom Peete Cross, a famous folklorist, which also made several references to witchcraft in Maryland that are helpful to our understanding of the topic.

Mention had been made previously about witches and their inability to cross over brooms. Cross wrote that "In many sections, including the highlands of the South, a broom laid across the doorway is sufficient protection [from witches] the true explanation of its value being that offered in Maryland: the witch cannot enter until she has counted all the straws of which the broom is made."[176]

While all of the accounts and stories so far regarding witchcraft were from either southern Maryland or the eastern shore, western Maryland was not immune from superstition. The author wrote that "[a]mong the white population of the Alleghany Mountains witches kill cattle by shooting them with balls of hair, and in western Maryland "witches' bullets" of pith or hair are often found in the bodies of dead animals."[177]

One might be tempted to think that the "witches bullets" found were merely hairballs left by cats or pellets left by birds after feasting on the animals that they had caught and consumed in the field.

Cross also gives rather strange and somewhat amusing story from Frederick in western Maryland. We are told that, "[a] miller in Frederick County, Maryland, who was troubled with nightmare, decided that his nocturnal visitor was a witch and accordingly one night stopped the keyhole of his room. Next morning he found a beautiful girl cowering in the cupboard. After keeping the maiden for some time as a servant, he married her. For several years the captive remained a dutiful and apparently contented wife, but on discovering one day that the keyhole had been unstopped, she escaped."[178]

It is hard to believe that anything like this actually happened. Perhaps he got into a fight with his wife and killed her and had to come up with an explanation for where she went after he disposed of the body. Or maybe it is just a tall tale and nothing more.

70

There were apparently other ways of stopping witches besides kidnapping and marrying them. Salt was also effective. "In western Maryland a witch is rendered powerless if salt is sprinkled under her chair...."[179] The author tells this tale about witches in Baltimore and how they were stopped: "In a story told by a negress in Baltimore, Maryland, two white ladies of apparently irreproachable life who were wont to slip out of their skins and sally forth nightly and who were not cured of their shape-shifting propensities until salt was rubbed on their raw hides, always assumed the form of cats before scampering up the chimney."[180]

If throwing salt was not your preference, image magic or witch-craft could also be used to seek revenge. The author observed that "[i]n western Maryland shooting the hag's picture with a bullet made from a silver coin is an effective means of retaliation."[181]

Many other traditions and legends regarding witchcraft are sure to exist in Maryland, especially in the small towns and rural areas. Dark secrets and mysteries relating to witchcraft that have not always been reduced to writing still exist. New legends, histories, and traditions may still be developing. The reader need only to seek out such tales on his own in order to be rewarded with the never-ending folklore on this subject.

Chapter 6
Newspaper Accounts of Witches and Witchcraft in the 19th and early 20th Centuries.

Newspaper accounts from the 19th and early 20th century give us a picture of how witchcraft was viewed by government, the mainstream society, and various others in Maryland and nearby areas at the time. Sorcery was no longer a felony and after Kilty reworked Maryland law after the Revolution, pretending to be a witch was no longer even a misdemeanor, although laws against fraud and disturbing the public peace still existed. Nevertheless, there were opportunities for mischief among those who either believed in the occult or sought to stir up others who did.

This author has researched local stories involving witchcraft in the archives of local papers through the online database provided by the Baltimore County Public Library. All stories were transcribed by this author from the non-OCR PDF files. Any mistakes are the fault of this author. The relevant and interesting results are placed in chronological order. It should be noted that some of the language is offensive to the modern reader, but that cannot be helped. By reading the articles we can experience the same thing that the people who initially read the articles did at the time they were published. We can have a unique look at the world as it existed then and see what the people of the time thought of witchcraft. Some of the articles regarding Baltimore will also suggest a new meaning behind Baltimore's nickname of *Charm City*.

The articles republished, up until 1916, are in the public domain.

From March 3, 1838 there is an article in *The Baltimore Sun* titled "The March of Mind" that sarcastically attacks witchdoctors. The authors wrote:

> Witchcraft. An instance of ignorant credulity and bare faced imposition has been related to us, which shows that our friends down east are not the only persons in this enlightened age who have been mystified by animal magnetism, Dr. John Williams, and other humbuggery. We of this good city can boast of having among us men of such rare endowments that they can drive out evil spirits from the being possessed, avert the malign influence of the evil eye, and break the spell laid on the pining babe by malicious beldames who fly by night on broom stick nags to crack a joke with Old Nick, and have a waltz with his imps in a grave yard; in short, they can perform any thing miraculous but make the banks resume specie payments, or teach the street loungers good manners. Sometimes, however, their exorcisms fail, and the less profound science of the regular physician effects a cure, as in the present instance, after the witch doctor has "given the patient up." A poor German woman, had a female child who from the hour of her birth appeared to be in constant agony. Something unnatural evidently affected the child, and to discover that something a celebrated witch doctor, named Shingle, was sent for. In due time the learned pundit made his appearance, and with the solemnity becoming one who wrestled with the foul fiend, he gazed upon the child and then shook his head, and the terror-stricken parents eagerly demanded what it mean. The sage, grave man, informed them that the infant was bewitched by the spells of some evil-disposed person who had a spite against the mother. He had seen such cases before, and had cured them for nothing, but he must be paid this time, for he did not like to leave his home without compensation, he would therefore only charge them five dollars, in advance, for relieving the child from malevolent influences, and send witches and witchcraft, hobgob-

blins and demons to the bottom of the Red Sea. The money was paid, and the learned Theban commenced his exorcism. What potent charms he employed or mysterious rites he performed, we are unable to say, but believe that some characters of magical import were inscribed over the door, through the influence of which the witch or wizard would be compelled to visit the house, and would be known to be the first person who entered the door, unbidden. The child, however, grew worse, and a regular physician was called in, who on examination found that the poor infant was laboring under a congenital malformation of the lumbar region. An operation was performed by the physician and the child is now doing well. The witch doctor was compelled to refund the five dollars, by a warrant being taken out against him for the amount, upon which he acknowledged judgment.

Now that we are on the subject of witchcraft, we think we could point out to the worthy exorcist some subjects for the exercise of his abilities. Numbers of young men may be seen about town who are certainly bewitched, demented or daft. On a fine day, when Market street is thronged with ladies, and a man of susceptible heart is bewildered by the witchery of thousands of bright eyes and lovely faces, these poor unfortunates may be seen standing in crowds at the corners of the streets, basking in the sun, and with rueful countenances peering beneath the bonnet and gazing upon the beauteous face of every lady who passes, as though they would fain discover the [unintelligible] ones whose charms have turned their reads. Another evidence of their being "possessed" is that on a Sunday they cannot enter a church, but cluster around the doors until the service is over, and then stare every female out of countenance, nay, we have known some to carry this mental hallucination so far as to speak to a strange lady in quite an endearing manner, thereby running an imminent risk of having his nose tweaked or his head broken by her justly incensed brother or husband. Now if any witch doctor or "powwower" can break the spell which binds these infatuated young men, his art will rank as a science with animal magnetism, and he himself be exalted in a niche in the Temple of Fame by the side of the Chevalier John Williams, Occultist to the King of the French.[182]

Elected government officials, journalists, and other influential professions, no longer believed that witchcraft had any real power, however, the less educated remained more susceptible to witch doctors and witches.

A *Baltimore Sun* article from April 1, 1839 states what happened the previous day in Baltimore City Court when a Judge Worthington had the docket. One entry stands out:

> Eliza Howard, a black, accused Rachael Cooper and Emma Trott, of having beaten her, but it appeared that she made the first a-sault by throwing salt in the face of Mrs. Cooper, who she believed to be a witch, and took that means of destroying the potency of her spells. Mrs. Cooper assured his honor that she was no such thing, for she did not believe in it, and she was therefore allowed to depart.[183]

First, nice pun—"a-sault". By the way, have you noticed how witches really don't like salt? Does Satan have high blood pressure or something? Or is it just the witches who are trying to avoid retaining water? Seriously however, salt was thought to protect against attacks by witches and it was often used by the superstitious.

Regarding the printing of the article on April 1, this could lead to speculation that this was part of an April Fool's joke at *The Sun*. However, there is no indication that this is the case and the story fits with what many people believed at the time and the general superstitions about witchcraft.

A classified ad that ran numerous times in *The Sun*, including on April 24, 1860, advertised the services of a conjurer and witch. The ad read:

> Dr. Samuel Funterbaugh, the most wonderful Astrologist and Phrenologist in the world, can now be found at his residence, No. 7 Fountain Street, between Alaxander and Fleet sts. He uses all kind of Witchcrafts and conjuring; cures all diseases and

spells; does anything wished for by the Ladies and Gentlemen; and anything that is stolen or lost returned by witchcraft or conjuring; or describe the person that does anything and give any person love that wants it. Fells Point.[184]

If you visit this area today the street numbers have all changed so you can't find where exactly he lived, but there are some nice townhouses there. Still, it is a relatively obscure place for someone with his talent to live. One would think that someone with his skills would have lived on a big estate, not in a small townhouse in Baltimore. It seems odd as well that someone with the good doctor's alleged abilities has been forgotten.

Witchcraft was certainly not unique to Maryland. *The Sun* reported on August 10, 1872 about an incident in South Carolina that the editor felt would be of interest to readers in the Baltimore area:

Rowdyism in South Carolina—The Sumter (S.C.) News says that a few nights ago a band of disguised negroes, in the upper part of the county, seized a colored man, whom they charged with being a Voodoo or witch doctor, cut one of his ears off, and then beat or whipped him most unmercifully. They alleged that he had already slain thirty negroes by his potent spells, and swore that they would stop his operations.[185]

The popular conception of Voodoo is similar or the same as Hoodoo, the term used by mainly blacks, Africans and Haitians, to describe the type of magic practiced by witches and witch doctors. The terms witch and witch doctor are often used interchangeably, although the term witch doctor could be used to describe someone who used witchcraft to counter-act the effects of a malicious witch.

Many Marylanders today have moved to southern Pennsylvania for lower taxes and cheaper real estate, but still work and have ties to Maryland. For that reason, this story reported in *The Washington Post* in an article titled "A Murderous Monomaniac" on July 28, 1884 will be of interest. The article read:

Philadelphia, July 27—A special dispatch to the Press from York, Pa., says Mrs. Adam Miller was shot through the body last night while sitting at a window of her father's residence, about five miles from York, holding her sick infant in her lap. The ball penetrated the lungs, and she will probably die. The shooting is supposed to have been done by Pius Miller, a brother of her husband. The husband, who was in the room at the time, ran to his wife's assistance and gave the alarm, but the guilty person had escaped in the darkness. Adam Miller to-day had a warrant issued for his brother's arrest, but the latter has not been seen since the shooting. Pius Miller has always been considered a monomaniac upon the subject of witchcraft, and upon several occasions it is stated that he has threatened his sister-in-law's life for "having bewitched him."[186]

This author could not find if Pius Miller was ever captured or convicted of this alleged crime. Although it may look suspicious, one would think that a jury would need more evidence in order to convict a person of murder. No one appears to have witnessed the killing and there is no hint of forensic evidence. If captured, hopefully Pius was wise enough to avoid giving a statement to the authorities.

Washington, D.C., the capital city of the United States, sits on land that once belonged to Maryland.[187] Sharing much of the culture and history of Maryland, it is worth considering some stories from there in this chapter. An article titled "a Negro and a Hoodoo Doctor: Mr. Williams Loses His Money Through His Superstition" from the September 6, 1885 edition of *The Washington Post* provides this story which is both comical and sad. According to *The Post*:

An old and honest-looking colored man was standing on the corner of Massachusetts avenue and K street north-west yesterday afternoon when a young and well-dressed darkey approached and said in tones indicative of great delight:

"Why Mr. Williams, how glad I am to see you! How are you getting along?"

Mr. Williams did not recollect ever having seen the man before, but feeling flattered at the friendly interest which was manifested, received his new friend with open arms, and in a few moments was engaged in unburdening himself to him. It seems that Mr. Williams had $10 with which he was going to pay his rent, but as there was $20 due he had devoted all the early part of the day to useless speculation as to where the rest of the money was coming from. He now appealed to his new acquaintance for advice which might assist him out of his predicament.

"Why, my dear fellow," said his friend, when the old man had finished his story, "nothing could be easier. Just place your money in this handkerchief," drawing one from his pocket, "I place this paper over it, tie it in a knot and in two hours it will double itself."

Wondering at the strange process for making money, but confident of the result, Mr. Williams did as he was bid. His younger companion covered the money carefully with a piece of paper, pronounced a few cabalistic words over it, tied the handkerchief in a knot, then handed it to the old man. "Now mind," he said, "don't open it for two hours," and, with an affectionate farewell, withdrew.

Mr. Williams stood for a few moments watching his friend's retreating figure, then returned slowly to his home, rejoicing at his good fortune. Before the two hours had elapsed, however, his curiosity overcame his scruples and he opened the handkerchief. Instead of twenty dollars, which he expected to find inside it, there was only a piece of paper.

His money was gone. Half frantic he rushed from the house and started in search of the thief; but after wandering about for an hour or two he became discouraged and reported the matter to the police.

Williams is now somewhat in doubt as to whether his money was really stolen or whether he prevented the transformation by being too precipitate in opening the handkerchief. He is very

79

anxious, however, to see the young man, if only to have the matter explained.[188]

Even after being taken advantage of by a con-man, this poor guy still continued to believe in the power of witchcraft and magic.[189] Although one might speculate that Mr. Williams never had any encounter with this mysterious man, but instead spent his money on drinks and dice, and made up this story and filed a false report in hopes of getting a break from his landlord. That probably isn't the case but things like that have been known to happen. The man, however, does not sound smart enough to think up such a plan. His story, sad as it is, is most likely true.

Hoodoo also made its way into the court system in Washington, D.C. On September 10, 1885 *The Post* published "Bits of Local News" that also included this blurb:

> In the case of William J. Armstrong, charged with libeling Dr. Wm. H. Hale, by calling him a hoodoo doctor, in the Police Court yesterday, Judge Snell refused to hear testimony as to the truth of the libel. The case went over until 1 o'clock to-day.[190]

The result of the trial was not given in this edition and does not appear to have been reported at any time. Whether the allegation from Armstrong was that Hale was actually a witch doctor or just a simple quack, is not known. Either could have been the case.

Back into Maryland, we are reminded that belief in witchcraft in the 19th century was not entirely confined to the poor and ignorant. On November 30, 1886, this amusing article, titled "Witchcraft and Spells" appeared in *The Sun*:

> A young girl applied to Justice Warfield yesterday for some legal advice. She said she had gone to a woman to cure her of a spell which had been put on her by some unknown enemy. The justice looked at the girl in surprise. She appeared to be intelligent, her dress, while not rich, was very neat and in good taste, and her

language was good. It is an ordinary thing for colored people and ignorant white people to worry the justice with yarns about spells and "conjurations," but here was a young girl, evidently educated and apparently refined, acknowledging her belief in spells. She laid down a bundle of hair which the woman had given her, telling her at the same time that it had been brought to her by the enemy who had put the spell on the girl. The person who brought the hair had been forced to do so by the old witch "putting a spell" on her without her knowledge. The gist of the young lady's complaint was that she had paid about $25 to the old woman to take the spell off and make her well, and that she wasn't free from the spell because she felt ill. Therefore she wanted $15 back. Justice Warfield asked her if the old woman was a fortune-teller, for only against these persons can the criminal law be invoked. "No sir," replied the young lady, "she is not a fortune-teller. She is a "mediator" or "moderator" I think she said." The girl doubtless meant "medium," but this was the only flaw in all her conversation. The justice explained to her that since the woman was not a fortune-teller, the only way to get the $15 was by a suit for damages. The young girl thanked him for his advice very politely, and then added, as she left the room: "I'm afraid to do that, sir: she might lay a spell on me." Justice Warfield did not try to argue with her about the "spell."[19]

It may seem odd that the girl was only asking for $15 back when the woman took $25, but from my scan of the article that appears to be the case, although it is slightly blurry. Perhaps the girl felt the woman deserved some compensation for trying. It is obvious from the story that the judge, while finding this slightly amusing, had no interest in seeing that anything was done in this situation. While there may have been laws against telling fortunes for money there were not laws against taking money to undo spells and none of it was a priority for the courts.

Some timeless political humor is always appropriate. The following blurb appeared in *The Post* on September 21, 1890:

A Place for the Hoodoo

From the Pioneer Press

"Washington," says a current paragraph, "is becoming noted for its 'hoodooed' houses. A number of the finest old residences in the city are unoccupied because they are believed to be 'hoodooed.'" What a blessing for the country it would be were the House of Representatives thus "hoodooed!"[192]

Apparently there were many nice vacant houses in the District because the locals believed that they were bewitched. Whether or not that was really the reason they were unoccupied is unknown. Many blacks and poor whites living there believed in witchcraft. The "finest old residences" were not likely occupied by them. Perhaps it was a situation no different from what we see in cities like Baltimore or D.C. today where what used to be nice houses have been abandoned due to urban blight. Or perhaps, like we suffer from in contemporary times, there was a depression in the housing market. Regardless of the reason, we are all still waiting for Congress to become hoodooed.

Staying in with politics, this blurb on January 4, 1891, from *The Post* also makes light of hoodoo superstitions:

Hon. Smith M. Weed evidently takes stock in the hoodoo theory. He will open his Senatorial campaign on the 13th.[193]

Running for the New York seat, Weed lost.

Law enforcement during the 19th century had their hands full dealing with some superstitious people. An article in *The Post* titled "Capt. Russ as a Hoodoo; Some Superstitions of Colored People Confined in the Jail" published on August 5, 1891 told the following stories about the D.C. Jail:

"No! no! no! Don't put me in the chapel! Please don't! I'll be good!"

A colored woman muffled in a blanket, her limbs writhing and twisting as she struggles to escape, shrieks this as she is borne across the stone floor by two jail guards. She is a refractory female prisoner and she is almost beside herself with fear, not of any physical harm, but purely from superstition. Nowhere would the psychologist find a better field for studying superstitions than in the jail. A large proportion of the prisoners are densely ignorant colored men, and in the negro race superstition is apt to be in an exaggerated inverse ratio to intelligence and education.

Warden Burke and all the other jail officials say that their most troublesome prisoners are the colored women, and naturally they are the most superstitious. The only form of punishment they fear in the least when they are crazy with anger is "the chapel." This is a large room over the kitchen, a sort of loft, without windows, and dark and gloomy. It is used principally for the storage of lumber and odds and ends of all sorts, and when the scaffold is taken down it is hidden away in there. For some reason that would probably puzzle these women themselves to state they have an abject horror of being left alone in this room. It is in a disconnected wing of the jail and silent as a grave.

No one knows why it is called the chapel, though it probably gets its name from the fact that the uncovered inside of the sharp peaked roof gives it a resemblance to the frequent form of real chapels. Often the female prisoners have quarrels among themselves or defy the matron's authority. The guards say that sometimes these hardened women work themselves into such a rage that their kinky hair stands out from their heads and they use language almost inconceivably vile. It is not safe even for the matron to approach them under these circumstances, and the guards have to be called on.

The regular form of punishment, handcuffing a refractory prisoner to the bars, usually has little effect on one of the enraged women. A favorite ruse with these women, when the matron calls for the guards in aid in subduing them after the violation of the rules is to remove every article of clothing. This is often effective in keeping the men from interfering.

But frequently an enraged woman will scream and blaspheme so horribly that it is absolutely necessary to subdue her. Then two of the guards get a blanket, and, unlocking the cell where the frenzied women is confined, wrap her in the blanket, handcuff her, and then carry her to the chapel. Once inside that she is silent.

Her rage is replaced by terror that is almost pitiful. Half an hour in the chapel is usually enough to bring the female prisoner to terms. A week on dry diet, as bread and water are called, after her half hour in the chapel, will probably make the woman a quiet, tractable prisoner for a couple of months.

All this applies to the colored women only. What few white women get into the District jail are not of the sort to be scared by an empty room, and they rarely need punishment. When they do a threat of a "dry diet" usually brings them to terms.

One of the most peculiar of the jailbirds' superstitions centers in Capt. Russ for many years the deputy warden of the jail, and the man for whom the prisoners come nearest to entertaining affection. They all look up to him and often ask his advice about all sorts of personal matters. He takes an interest in such of the prisoners as show a disposition to do right and encourages them. Much as the prisoners like him, and some of the habitual lawbreakers know him very well, no experienced criminal will shake hands with Capt. Russ or allow the captain to touch him as he is leaving jail after serving out his sentence, if he can avoid it.

The superstitious prisoners believe that if Capt. Russ touches them they will be brought back again, as they say Capt. Russ is a "hoodoo." Often as a negro stands before the heavy oaken front door of the jail, eager to inhale his first breath of free air since the commission of some crime against life or property, Capt. Russ approaches, holding out his hand, and says:

"Now, my boy, try and stay away from here,"

And the prisoner will answer, edging away from the outstretched hand.

"Deed I will cap'n, but ef yo' touches me I'll haf ter come back sho', whether I does anything or not. 'Scuse me, cap'n."

So general has this belief become among the colored prisoners that Warden Russ rarely essays to shake hands with a prisoner when he is about to regain his liberty.

Another peculiar superstition jailbirds have is concerning rats. A prisoner thinks that if he succeeds in capturing a rat he is sure to regain his liberty. If he is in jail awaiting trial he regards it as an augury that he will be acquitted. If he is convicted he expects either to find an opportunity to escape or that some miraculous legal chicanery on the part of his lawyer will free him. The truest optimist is the jailbird.[194]

Belief in superstitions, witchcraft, and hoodoos was not limited to the lower class black people. "Thinks it is a Hoodoo," was an article published in *The Post* on August 15, 1891. Again, keep in mind that the language is from the time. According to the reporter:

Estella Lucas, a very intelligent and attractive mulatto girl, is the cause of a sensation among the colored people of southwest Washington. The girl claims that her aunt tried to poison her because she wanted to marry, and the aunt states positively that the girl has been hoodooed and has lost her senses.

Thursday, the young girl with a lady by whom she is employed, went to the Fourth precinct station and reported that her aunt, Mrs. Bessie Davis, living at 427 E Street southwest, had tried to poison her and that her wedding-day was set for yesterday.

She gave as her reason for believing that her aunt had administered poison that she was opposed to marriage and had said she would dose her before she should marry the young man to whom she was engaged.

"I know," said the girl, "that she tried to poison me because I had carried home some whisky, and when I drank some it seemed like my stomach was on fire and burning up. She put something in it to kill me, so I couldn't marry Fred Simpson."

Sergt. Barry looked into the case and found that the bottle in which the whisky had been put had been used as a camphor bottle, and that it had not been thoroughly cleansed before the whisky was put in. He also ascertained that the girl's aunt was one of the oldest and best known colored women in South Washington, and had spent many years of hard toil raising the girl, who was left in her keeping when a babe.

Mrs. Davis lives in a comfortable house, nicely furnished, and to a Post reporter she said:

"Estella has left my house, and gone to live at a Mrs. King's. She is now nearly twenty years old, and was left in my yard by my sister when she was not more than two years old. I worked hard to take care of her, and gave her a good education. She was bright and smart and learned fast, and I was proud of her, the Lord knows. Up to a few months ago Estella was a dutiful girl, but she met a young nigger named Fred Simpson, who put a spell on her. I believe he hoodooed her, because she just moped around, and would sit at the window looking for him for hours. I never did like Simpson because he plays a guitar and never works. He always appears to have plenty of money and everybody says he does not work. How he managed to put such a spell over my girl Estella I do not know. But he simply ran her crazy. Thursday she came home and packed up her clothes and moved to Mrs. King's. She would never have done this if the spell had not been put on her by that young fellow Simpson. The Lord knows I never thought of trying to poison her, but I expect she would be better off dead than living under the spell Simpson has placed on her. I cannot sleep for thinking of how my child has been taken from me by that fellow.[195]

The woman almost certainly was innocent of poisoning the girl, but one could still speculate.

Sometimes the law enforcers themselves were superstitious. The light-hearted article titled "Hoodoos for a hobby; Superstitions Prevalent Among Some Members of the Police Force. Officer Dyer's Observations; Connection a Call for the Patrol Wagon with a Black Cat—Crap-Shooters and Wife-Beaters-Lieut. McCathran's Cigar a Jo-nah" from *The Post* on on November 1, 1891 tells us that:

> There are not many people nowadays who believe in "hoodoos," but there are a few who are convinced of the existence of such beings, and wonder where and what that article is, which appears to be invisible and intangible, but, to use a strict phrase, "gets there all the same."

> Perhaps there is not a man connected with the police force who is a greater believer in "hoodoos" than Bob Dyer, who has charge of the patrol service of the Fifth Precinct. He tells some wonderful stories of "hoodoos," and often at night will sit around the station and spin such remarkable yarns that some of the more nervous officers become almost afraid to go to their beds in the dormitory. Some of them believe Bob to be the second Munchhausen, but such is not the case. He is honest and sincere in what he believes and says, and does not like to have anyone doubt him.

> "If, for instance," he said to a Post reporter, while sitting in the station, "this bell rings and the patrol wagon is called for a plain drunk, just as sure as fate a black cat will cross the street in front of the horse before we get back to the station. It is no use to unhitch the horse, for we will have another call of a similar character before six hours roll around. Never knew it to fail, and, by George, the blotter will substantiate what I say, and——"

> "About the black cat, too?" interrupted the reporter.

> "No, not that, but I'll vouch for the cat story. Fact, every word of it. Now, here's another thing. If a man gets his leg crushed in this precinct we may always hear of another within the next twenty four hours, and in nine cases out of ten the second one appears on time. Why this is so I cannot explain, but it is true. Yes, I am a believer in 'hoodoos' but I don't like the black-cat attachment.

That could be done away with very easily, and it would not look so much like the work of the devil."

"When a crap-shooter is brought in I just put myself in readiness to go out and bring in some fellow who has filled up on coffin varnish and has tried to whip his wife or did do it. This never fails, and I will bet a $5 note on it any time any one has that amount to lose. No, it does not work the other way. If a wife beater is brought in first, a crap-shooter will not be arrested for a month, no matter how diligent the officers may be or how numerous the shooters. Again, let a pugnacious negro stick his knife or razor into another colored brother, and in less than seven hours an officer will apply for a sick card, and it is generally about five days before he is ready again for duty. On the other hand, if an officer applies for a sick card, the fire alarm will be sent in within thirteen hours. Whether it means that the officer is going to die and go where the bells don't ring I do not know.

"But the funniest hoodoo I know of did not appear until Lieut McCathran took charge of this precinct. Whenever he comes up the steps and throws down a stump of a cigar on the pavement the patrol wagon will be called out within five hours to bring in an injured man. I have made a study of these things, but I can't tell why they happen, and I would like very much to meet the man who can. People who want may laugh and call it foolishness and superstition, but it is true—my word, I have told you. No ghost stories or spirit rappings will go down with me, but I do believe in 'hoodoos'—the very biggest kind of a believer."[196]

This was a strange article and not expressly about witchcraft, but it does show that many superstitions were held by some police officers.

Not even the White House or the police officers stationed there were immune from the superstition of the area. An article titled "Trouble with Reptiles, An Athletic Negro Crank Storms the White House. Wanted His Hoodoo Off" published in *The Post* on July 2, 1893 informs us that:

Private Secretary Thurber was last night given his first experience of the native born crank of the more buoyant and flamboyant type.

A little before 8 o'clock a negro man, over six feet in height, of some 200 pounds weight and proportionately muscular, entered the White House and demanded an interview with the President. According to his statement he had something much more serious the matter with him than a thirst for office.

His voice was filled with anguish as he recited how he had been employed at the Executive Mansion by President Grant; how while drawing his salary and accumulating fat he had been hoodooed, and how this enchantment had taken the horrible form of reptiles imbedded and living under the skin.

"I has one snake in mer foot," he said, "an' I cals Peter; dar's anuder in mer lef' breas' an' I calls him Moses. As fur frogs an' lizards, so many on 'em runs aroun' in mer lef' laig dat I ain't got no time to name 'em. Gin'ul Grant sent me down Souf' fur to get de cha'm wucked off and de people sent me on to Spain. Pres'dent Cleveland am de only man what kin fetch 'em out'n me. Whah is he at?"

Officer Hardy, one of the Metropolitan policemen regularly detailed at the White House, told the strange visitor that the President had gone out of the snake-charming business temporarily, and was not in town anyhow. The negro, who had interjected a statement that his name was John Stevens, reached out for Hardy. Officer Parker, who was standing near took a hand, and the fun began. The negro became maniacal. The two men opposed to him are by no means children, but for a quarter of an hour he gave them all that they could attend to.

His "wind" was remarkable, as during the entire struggle he did not cease for a moment to yell at the top of his voice and swear with a fluency and completeness that proved he had lived in more than one country, whether Spain is on the list or not. They got him out on the portico a wild tangle of legs and arms and lungs, and he got himself back inside with apparently as little effort as is expended in using up a stock of sugarcane. The performance was repeated until the officers began to think that they had died and been sentenced to wrestle through all eternity with an ebony phantom filled with snakes, frogs, lizards, and every other reptilian thing in creation.

The snake in his left foot seemed to have gifted him with surprising suppleness; "Moses," who dwells in his left side, had added calluses to him, and every one of the frogs, to numerous to name had lent him the power to hop about like an insane jumping-jack. When the contest was at its height Secretary Thurber came down stairs and said:

"What! what! what's the matter?"

The afflicted African instantly stopped his terrific yells for "Gen'ul Cleveland" and looked at the secretary in an aimless and stupid manner. The moment, however, that the latter began to ascend to his big room he began with redoubled ardor, and the fun was once more fast and furious. In the meantime another of the employees had rung for a police wagon and it came. Stevens by super-human efforts was loaded into it. Its only occupant, other than the driver was Officer Gaucher. To him the man with the hoodoo transferred his attentions. They had it all of the way to the Third precinct station. It took half of the force to land him in the cell, and at an early hour this morning he was still demanding admittance to "de only man what kin fetch'em out'n me."[197]

It almost sounds like the man was under the influence of Phencyclidine, or PCP, which this author has noticed is popular with many of the poor and disadvantaged in the greater D.C. area, but this is impossible as the substance had not been invented yet.[198] Perhaps he was under the influence of some other drug, such as cocaine, or had a mental illness. Or perhaps the man actually did believe that he had been subjected to some form of bewitching and was driven mad by it. One hopes that he eventually got some help for his problems.

Going back into Maryland proper, *The Sun* published an article titled "Maryland Folklore; Odd Customs, Superstitions, and the Beliefs in the State; Some Spells and Charms" on August 25, 1899 that addressed those witchcraft inspired topics. According to *The Sun*:

Miss Annie Weston-Whitney, secretary of the Maryland Folklore Society, who is spending this part of the summer at Everett, Pa., writes THE SUN as follows about folklore in Maryland:

"Once more Maryland comes to the front and stands unrivaled. This time she is proving herself a storehouse for rare bits of superstitions and beliefs that are of value to the scientist who studies man through his customs, superstitions, and beliefs. The fact is being generally recognized that many of these same traditions, familiar to all have been handed down from generation to generation since the beginning of history and a careful study of them helps to throw light on the origin and history of customs and observances.

"Various causes have combined to render Maryland a favorite spot for the growth and preservation of much of this traditional lore. Add to this that which is local, or native to the soil, and it becomes doubtful if any other part of the country can furnish so much material of this kind at first hand. It is difficult, however, to recognize the value of what is part of one's everyday life. It is a constant repetition of the story of the man who left his home and went to seek for diamonds, and returned after a total failure to find that another had sought them on his property and found 'acres of them.' It is also difficult to point out special features in one's own everyday life that are not common to all those living under the same form of government.

"Some of the good people of our State would doubtless be surprised to find how simple a chance expression betrays the birthplace. They would also find it difficult to believe that the moon could influence the demand for certain articles in Lexington Market, or that a superstitious belief could in any way affect the standing of the State as the 'gastronomic' one. Yet numerous incidents could be quoted that would point to these facts.

"A young lady summering on the Massachusetts coast was calling a little boy, and not being able to attract his attention at once called several times:

"'Harry! O, Harry! Harry! O, Harry!'

"A gentleman living near Boston lifted his hat and said: 'Miss Baltimore, will you kindly tell me where I can find the landlady?'

"'How did you know I was from Baltimore?' asked the girl, looking into the face of a perfect stranger.

"'Your speech betrayed you,' he said.

"'It was the use of the 'O,' with the rising inflection.

Market and Kitchen Superstition

"Crabbers and fisherman in our State assert that hard crabs have more meat in their shells during the increase than the decrease of the moon, and some of our housekeepers are now making the same assertion, and are only buying them in market on the 'increase of the moon.'

"If one were to undertake to collect the customs and folklore gathered about our market alone, they would reap a rich harvest. The day has not entirely passed when the housekeeper who does her own marketing arranges spring and fall for her 'market bonnet' and her 'market dress'—terms that would need an interpreter in New England or even in parts of Pennsylvania, where it is the 'scuff hat' that is trimmed to 'go scuffing in,' which, being interpreted, means to go on errands.

"From the market to the kitchen is but a step and there we find that superstition is responsible for the loss to the world of recipes for dishes that have been celebrated in connection with certain famous Maryland cooks. Who does not know of futile efforts to procure recipes from these queens of the kitchen? The apparent willingness was always there, but the result would be something like this:

"'Now, Auntie, I would like you to tell me just how you make those delicious muffins.'

"'Cert'nly, honey, cert'nly: fust I takes my flour -'

"'How much flour, Auntie?'

"'Das 'cordin ter how many muffins I'se gwine ter make honey. Ef I wants more muffins, I takes more flour: an' den I takes my aiggs -'

"Any one who has tried knows the futility of getting anything more definite: nor was this entirely from the fact, as some have asserted, that they did not 'measure things,' but from the belief as well that if they once gave away the recipe they would never succeed with it again themselves, or an enemy or witch might get hold of it and 'work a spell' on them.

"There is no stronger belief among this class of people that an enemy, by getting hold of something belonging to them, can 'conjure' them. As a rule a 'witch doctor' when asked to work a spell on a person, will ask at once for something belonging to him. From the frequency of its use, we might suppose that a lock of hair was the most effective thing to use in either working 'on' or 'off' a 'spell.' Those who are familiar with a recent case in Baltimore, where a man and wife professed to have been 'spelled' may have noticed the use of the lock of hair.

Use of Hair to Work Spells

"We are told, therefore, in Maryland that 'you must never let the combings of your hair fly out the window, for the birds may get them and build their nests with them, when you would have headache as long as the nests last, or a witch might get them and conjure you.' Again, it is claimed that if your enemy can plug a bit of your hair up in a tree. If it is only a little, you will have a headache, but if it is a large lock, you will go 'favin' structed. I was told of one case of this kind where the owner had almost lost her mind, when lightning struck the tree and freed the hair, and the owner was cured.

"The use of hair in working 'on' and 'off' spells is very ancient: so that we find everywhere warnings as to the care of the cuttings and combings. In some places in Europe it is still recommended that they be either burned or buried, in others that they be burned or thrown into running water, lest the birds get them, and the rest of the hair fall out, or witches get them and harm the owner.

"The plugging of the hair in a tree has been used to cure diseases as well as to 'work spells.' In Hertfordshire, England, there was once an oak, standing near a certain crossroad, that was said to have the power of curing ague. The patient was taken to it, and a lock of his hair plugged in the tree and then wrenched from the head.

"Who has not been told that the hair must only be trimmed when the moon is on the increase. And how many there are who rigidly adhere to this, giving as a reason that it should be done just so often and it is easy to remember in that way. I have never heard or seen any more definite reason given for this until recently when a well-known hairdresser in Baltimore, after telling me she would under no consideration cut the hair at any other time, explained that there is an ebb and flow in the hair that is affected by the moon, just as the tides in the ocean. With the new moon, she explained, the sap begins to go up to the roots, and with the full moon it goes down again; so cutting then would be destroying the sap. The ancients believed that the hairs of the head were the means of ingress and egress of spirits to the brain; for this reason esthetics allowed the hair to grow long and would not disturb it lest thereby they disturb some bit of wisdom on its way to the head.

"It is believed in Maryland that if you put a horse's hair in 'good whisky,' it will turn into a snake. A colored woman told me she had seen it tried, and the snake was black, had a tail and 'wriggled.'

A Hoodoo Doctor's Handkerchief

"In Maryland it is believed that a witch or 'hoodoo doctor' has a certain amount of power over an individual, if something belonging to him is in the possession of the individual. A curious instance of this so-called hoodooism has occurred in our own State, the victim being a young lady, who is rather phlegmatic, something of a dreamer, with a nature free from excitability. Not far from her home lived an old 'witch doctor,' who was feeble, decrepit, dressed in rags and was noticeable for the red bandanna handkerchief he always wore around his neck. One day, while walking with some friends, the young lady discovered the handkerchief under a tree near the road, and stooped to pick it up. Her friends, who recognized it as well as she, protested, and drew her away. After she had gone on a little, however, she went back and again tried to secure it. A second time her horrified companions succeeded in drawing her way; but the third time she was successful, and carried it off, and would not be separated from it night or day, keeping it about her person during the day and sleeping with it under her head at night. It is said that from the moment she touched it her whole nature underwent a complete change. She began to waste away and would rise in the night and become greatly excited, crying and clasping the handkerchief closer to her. Any effort to get it away from her only excited her and increased the trouble. One night, however, her sister succeeded while she was asleep in taking it from under her head and burning it.

Immediately the girl began to improve, and before long was her old self; and her friends now speak of the whole affair as 'very queer.'

Holy Innocents' Day Unlucky

"Our Maryland negroes have preserved certain old customs that are hardly recognizable ones. There are those who will remember the time when a Maryland negro would not begin any work or do certain kinds on 'Chilmers Day.' Efforts would be made to finish some things or to begin others the day before, if it took till midnight, rather than be obliged to do them on 'Chilmers Day' which was in reality Childermas or Holy Innocents' Day, which, in the early church and long afterward, was looked on as an especially unlucky day. It was believed that the children slaughtered by Herod on that day did not go into Paradise, but into Limbo, where they had to wait the coming of the Redeemer, who opened the gates of Heaven. In Rome the day was observed as a day of mourning, and meat was forbidden. In Medieval England children were treated to a sound whipping in bed that morning 'that the memorie of this murther might stick the closer.'

"It was not only considered unlucky to commence anything on this day, but to put on new clothes, to pare the nails or even to wash on the same day of the week throughout the year. Louis XI would allow no mention in his presence of affairs of state on this day: while Edward IV, when he discovered that the date set for his coronation was December 28, Holy Innocents' Day, ordered the coronation postponed. Anything begun on Holy Innocents' day, it was been said, will never be finished; so when our Maryland negro began a piece of work the night before, that he might not have to do it on 'Chilmers Day,' he was only doing what had been done by his master and his master's ancestors.

Odd New Year's Morning Beliefs

"In Maryland again, we find methods of averting certain kinds of ill luck that do not seem to be found elsewhere. The significance of the 'first foot' is perhaps generally known. It is a very old belief that the luck of the year for each particular household is affected by the first foot that crosses the threshold on New Year's morning. A woman brings ill luck; in some parts of England it is believed that she represents death. A man brings luck, but there are gradations there, for a red-haired man is unlucky, and in some places a light-haired one is looked upon askance. It is the dark-haired man who brings the best luck, and in England it was at one time customary for dark-haired men to hire themselves out for liquor and an alms to be on hand at midnight to 'take the new year in.'

"Both in Scotland and in England the custom became general of keeping spiced ale, cakes and good cheer of various kinds for the 'first foot,' and the time of his appearance was as near midnight as possible. Sometimes a carol singer was captured and taken in the front door and out the back for luck and for this he was rewarded with a 'luck penny.' In some Maryland families the old custom that was general with the upper classes in England still prevails. Arrangements are made with a boy, the son of a friend or neighbor, to come to the house early in the morning before any one else. In Maryland, however, we find a way to 'cross the luck' should a woman come to the house first. It is done by taking her in 'kitchen way' but it is necessary that a member of the household should meet her outside and 'go in with her.'

"In Maryland it is asserted that the child born on New Year's Day must be carefully guarded, or 'it will not live the year out.'

Folklore Connected with Bread

"In the matter of charms and counter-charms, Maryland is prolific, nor is the use of them confined to any one class. We have recently had our attention attracted to the bread and butter cure for whooping cough by the way in which Mrs. Lloyd Downdes, our Governor's wife, because she is the mother of twins, has been called on to provide it. Maryland has another cure for the same disease that is somewhat similar. In this case it is a woman, who has married without changing her name, who has the power to effect the cure. The child who has whooping cough has only to go to her and ask her for bread and butter; if she spreads it herself, and the child takes it without thanking her, there will be no more whoop to that cough.

"Bread has an immense amount of folklore connected with it, and has been regarded as being possessed with certain occult powers that have caused it to be looked upon as almost sacred, certain ceremonies being connected with the dedicated of the bakeoven itself, as in Brittany, where, among other things, the breaking of an egg before it is first used is considered essential to good luck. There bread must never be baked on All Saints' day, for the ghosts will get it and eat it. The custom of carrying a crust of bread in the pocket as a charm is referred to by Herrick, when he says: 'If ye fear to be affrighted 'When by chance ye are benighted, 'In your pocket for a trust 'Carry nothing but a crust, 'For that holy piece of bread 'Charmes the danger and the dread.

Charms to Cure Infant Ills

"Attention has been drawn to another charm for the cure of infant ills, through the moles that infested Druid Hill Park in the spring. A man who was very successful in catching them made quite a little sum of money by selling the feet, which were cut off while the animals were still alive, to mothers who believed that by putting them in a bag and then hanging them around the necks of their children the disease that come with teething could be avoided. In some parts of this country the Molucca bean is worn in this way round the neck to protect children, and it is said that if evil threatens the child who wears one, the bean, which is red will turn black.

"Baltimore furnishes a variety of charms that are worn in this way; one for the cure of chills and fever is but a bit of writing on paper, that must never be looked at by the sufferer. Doubtless if he looked at it he would not understand it, for the wearing of written charms is very ancient, and the words were often unintelligible, but then they were intended for the spirits and they understand words that are perfectly unintelligible to human beings. The ancient Arabian used a certain kind of bean in this way for the protection of his camel. He would put 64 grains in a bag and 'with a fine linen thread suspended it round the neck' of his camel. This was supposed to keep the animal healthy and to ward off accidents.

"It is often asserted that it is only the ignorant and unlettered who are really superstitious, but Philadelphia has recently furnished us with an example of the hold certain popular superstitions have on the world at large, regardless of rank or education. During the time of the summer exit a certain gate in Broad street railroad station, leading to one of the popular outgoing trains, was not equal to the demand upon it, and to relieve the congestion a second gate was opened, but, to the surprise of the officials, only a few straggling tourists could be persuaded to make use of it, the others preferring to risk the loss of seat and train rather than on through a gate whose number, they could see, was 13. We all know how this unfortunate number is avoided, so that it is now rarely to be seen on the doors of hotel rooms or the state rooms of ocean steamers; while the feeling that it is unlucky or the sign of death to sit down to a meal with 13 at the table is familiar to everyone. In parts of England it is considered worse to do this on Saturday than any other time. In Maryland the result may be either death or a marriage, and this is so in Scotland as well.

"The ill luck of the number 13 seems to date from the Last Supper, and to have spread with Christianity. It neither was been nor is unlucky everywhere. In parts of the East and among our Indians we find it regarded as a sacred number. It stands with some Indians for perfection, completeness, representing the perfect man. And the Indian arrives at it in this way. He represents man first as standing on the earthly plane and taking in all space, which is represented first by the cardinal points—the east, the north, the west and the south—making four, and then the Above, the Below and the Here, or the man, making seven in all. Then he is represented as standing on the celestial plane, and again in space, represented by the four cardinal points named in the same order—only an evil spirit would name them in any other order—and the Above, the Below, but the Here or the man can only be counted once, so instead of twice seven, we have seven and six, making 13, the perfect man, which makes the number itself sacred."[199]

As this author wrote previously in this chapter, the story about the bizarre use of charms in Baltimore suggests a different meaning behind the city's nickname of *Charm City*. One certainly cannot think of a better reason why it should be called that.

William H Cooke

Belief in witchcraft was not limited exclusively to the black community, but was also strong among the immigrant class who brought to America with them their old world superstitions. In an article published on October 11, 1901, titled "Persecuted as a Witch" *The Sun* tells us this story about an incident in a Baltimore Courtroom:

> In the corner of Justice Sauber's court at the Southern Police Station yesterday afternoon sat an old woman with bowed head who sobbed as though her heart would break.
>
> "Oh, your Honor!" she cried in broken English when asked to state the cause of her grief. "I am called a witch."
>
> Becoming interested, the Justice looked at her most closely. Her form was bent and her face gashed by many scars, her eyes and nose being far from symmetrical and her appearance suggesting the traditional weaver of spells.
>
> "Judge," she continued, "my name is Cara Merklem and I live at 24 West Church street. I am not a witch, but a plain washerwoman. At 117 Hanover street there is a little Greek baby, the son of John Perdekac. The baby is dying, and I am accused of causing its death through the influence of my evil eye. During the past week I have been washing for Mr. John Props, who lives on the third floor of 117 Hanover street. The Perdekaes live on the first floor. Wednesday I went down to the first floor to get some irons. As I pass through the room of Perdekac the baby was on the floor. 'what a pretty baby!' I said, and took it up in my arms. Today I again passed through the room. I was grabbed by Mr. and Mrs. Perdekac. They cried, 'Oh, you witch! Our little baby is sick and dying and you with the evil eye are the cause. Yes, you! you! you!' And they shook me.
>
> "'Now,' they cried in chorus, 'you have got to spit in the face of the child.' I was horrified. The idea of spitting in the face of the little dear. I protested, but they threatened, and to gratify their whim I did spit in the face of the baby."

Justice Sauber remarked that he had heard of a superstition among the Greeks and other people of the Far East that a person can be injured by the influence of the "evil eye" and that spitting in the face of the injured person acted as an antidote.

"Now," continued the woman between sobs, "I am afraid the child will die anyhow and I will be blamed. They are fierce people, those Greeks. I don't know what will become of me. All day long the neighbors have been crying, 'There goes the witch, the woman with the evil eye. She can do anything. Say, witch, make me a thousand dollars, will you?' and all such things as that. I am followed by the children who have taken up the cry of their parents, and my life is miserable. I have been in this country 18 years and I have never been called a witch before. What am I to do?"

Justice Sauber remarked that there was nothing to be done and that the persecution would soon subside if she paid no attention to the cries.

Cara left the station, covering her head with a ragged shawl and muttering that she would go crazy if the people did not stop accusing her of supernatural powers.

Mrs. Perdekac's knowledge of English is very limited and she explained to a Sun reporter what she thought of the woman of the evil eye. Her husband, who is a banana peddler, was not at home. The baby, which is about 4 months old, was lying upon a rickety bed wrapped in a lot of old rags and seemingly very sick. The room did not present an inviting appearance.[200]

Witchcraft also found its way into the Baltimore courts when it was used as an excuse for crime, or at least mitigation, as it was in a 1902 case reported in *The Sun*. On August 5, 1902 in an article titled "Says He Couldn't be Good" was published. According to the reporter:

Negro Boy Blames Voodoo For his Lawless Propensities.

An entirely new version of the powers of a voodoo doctor was developed yesterday at the Northern Police Station, when Harry

Matthews, colored, was brought in by Patrolman Hartman on the charge of being incorrigible. He is the son of Daniel Matthews, 9 Belt street.

Harry is extremely small and very black, but is said to be able to produce more mischief than half a dozen ordinary youngsters. Many times he has caused great mental anguish to his father and invited corporal punishment by doing just exactly what he was most certain was entirely wrong. He devoted parent correct him with tongue and strap, but only wasted his energy by his campaign of judicial reform.

Yesterday Harry broke a street lamp. Then Matthews, Sr., determined that patience had ceased to be a virtue and had his young hopeful arrested on the charge of being a vicious minor.

At the station house Harry said in explanation of his troubles that he was bad, very bad, and that he knew it, but that it was because he was hoodooed. A woman with whom he was not acquainted had put a spell on him and it was impossible for him to be good. A colored woman in his neighborhood who was a "spiritualist and tended to fixing up speerits" told him that another colored woman had bewitched him, so that it was impossible for him to keep within the law.

Harry said that he was still under the spell and that as long as he could not reform until its baleful influence had died away he thought it would be well to lock him up in some institution where the witch could not get at him.

He will have a chance to make his explanation again to Judge Heuisler in the[201]

The article oddly ends there. One would imagine that the next word as "morning" or "afternoon". Whether or not the boy was telling the truth is a fair question. From the other stories we have seen that many people took hoodoo and witchcraft very seriously. It may be a plausible explanation that he acted as he did because he believed that he was under an evil influence.

Witch doctors were referenced for comedic purposes in this humorous articled titled "A Perennial Nuisance" from the October 15, 1908 edition of *The Sun*. The writers took issue with talent of England's Poet Laureate (would you expect to see such criticisms today in a mainstream publication?) and wrote:

Alfred Austin, Poet Laureate of England, has broken into print again. This time his contribution to the sublime store of Anglo-Saxon literature is a seven-stanza quasi-poem in F flat minor, in which he expresses the hope that his best girl (name unknown) will remember him after he is gone, and perchance shed a tear upon his lonely, grass-grown grave.

Alfred's reference to his grass-grown grave, we opine, is a mere figure of speech, intended to give proof of his shrinking modesty, for he is well aware that when measles at last lays him low or a long-suffering populace gathers at his home some dark night and lynches him—he is acutely aware, we maintain, that when this sad day arrives he will be entombed, not in a common cemetery, but in Westminster Abby. The venerable abby, despite the awe with which it is regarded by American tourists, shelters the bones of many such gilded no-bodies and pensioned vacuums, while Shakespeare is spending eternity on the banks of the Avon, Gordon is sleeping at Khartoum, where his work was done, and Darwin's immortal ashes are in some neglected corner.

When Tennyson died and it was in order to appoint a new poet laureate, the logical candidate, of course, was Rudyard Kipling. He was at the height of his fame then and his ringing versus was making the blood of all Britain leap. A plebiscite would have resulted in his election by an overwhelming majority. But Kipling, from the court standpoint, was not good metal for a poet laureate. He was altogether too daring, too truthful, too careless of the rights of rank and birth, too fond of singing the thing he saw it for the good of things as they were. He had preached a holy war upon sham and pretense, and he had written "The Widow at Windsor":

Walk wide o' the Widow at Windsor,
For 'alf o' creation she owns:
We 'ave bought 'er the same with the sword
an' the flame
An' we've salted it down with our bones,
(Poor beggers!—it's blue with our bones!)

This was ringing verse, perhaps, but it was also atrociously bad politics. So Kipling's name was scratched from the list of possible laureate.

How Austin came to be chosen is a problem that gives the historian pause. No doubt it was because he had the greatest pull at court. Whatever the reason, Alfred got the job, and he has been breaking into print now and again, ever since.

If we thought it would do any good, we would hire a St. Mary's county witch doctor to put a spell on him, and to make him pine away and hold his peace; but this, we are convinced, would be useless. The day after his funeral an even worse poet would be appointed to succeed him.[202]

Although the article is unsigned, one can almost picture H.L. Mencken sitting at a desk writing this diatribe. Whoever the writer, he believed and his readers must have believed that witch doctors still practiced their arts down in rural St. Mary's County. That seems appropriate as this was where Calvert's men first settled and where the early criminal cases involving witches were heard. St. Mary's County had and still has a large black population, but there is no reason to think that the witch legends and stories are limited only to them.

In the dark woods, on salty Chesapeake beaches, and in large tobacco (or whatever the hell they grow there now) fields of St. Mary's County, enough raw material is present to form in the mind of any person the superstitions and myths required for belief in witchcraft.

Going back again to western Maryland, *The Sun* reminded us in a January 31, 1909 article that superstition continued to play a role in daily life there as well. The article "Blue Ridge Mountaineers Who Still Believe in Witchcraft, Magic and Devils" starts with a historical inaccuracy (witches were not burned in English North America, but hanged) but otherwise provides information about the beliefs of people at the time in that area of the State. The reporter wrote:

Highfield, MD., Jan 30

Witch-Burning has been out of fashion in the United States for many years, but up here in the mountains witchcraft itself still has a host of devotees.

The most ignorant mountain folk are as superstitious as savages. Spells and incantations seem as real to them as orchards and horses.

Less than a year ago a 2-year-old child of a Blue Ridge mountaineer died from burns received while playing at a kitchen stove, because its parents failed to summon a physician (of whom there were two only a mile away) and placed their faith in a woman who was held in high awe in the neighborhood for her reputed ability to "blow for fire."

The Poor Child Died

The child was burned from head to foot, but all that was done for the suffering little creature was to summon an old and ignorant fraud. After several days the child's clothing was fast to raw flesh and a more enlightened neighbor timidly suggested that a "regular doctor" be summoned. He was summarily rebuked by the "fire-blower" and the child's parents. At the end of a week, however, the parent's evidently began to weaken in their faith of the quack's power and a licensed physician was sent for.

Upon his arrival he was horrified by the condition of the child. He exerted all his efforts to relieve its sufferings, but on the following day it died—a sacrifice to ignorant superstition. In a private conversation the doctor declared that he could have saved the child's life had he been summoned as soon as the "fire-blower." It is not known, however, that he called the attention of the authorities to the case.

The woman who did the "blowing-for-fire" act is a devout church member. Indeed, the mountaineer or "foot-hiller" and "valley-ite" is the exception who does not belong to some Christian church, and what is more, attend it far more regularly than does his average city brother.

Yet, despite all of this, ignorant superstition plays a most impor-tant part in the life of some of these people. There is scarcely an ailment or an ill without its charm or remedy. For serious cases there are voodoo specialists, of whom one may be "gifted" to "blow fire," which is a mysterious rite reputed to heal anything from bunions to tuberculosis, "pervided ever't'ing is jest right."

The Fire Blower

Thus while the magician who "blew for fire" in the child's case was a woman "highly esteemed" in her immediate community, only "a man who never saw his own father" can successfully "blow fire." It is not amiss to explain that a posthumous son is meant.

For the paraphernalia the "fire-blower" has only a piece of wood, said to have been chipped from the most inaccessible hickory tree on the mountain top, an enormous amount of ludicrous im-portance, a hypocritical air of mystery and a comic opera dignity.

The "fire blower" never gives a public performance. His rites are practiced in private only the patient (or victim to be more accu-rate) as a witness. The victim has impressed upon him by the op-erator, too, that unless he maintains the most absolute secrecy regarding the details of the "fire-blowing" turn, all the operator's powers will be in vain, and the sufferer will be stricken with a worse affliction. Thus, all one knows about the "fire-blower" is that he lights his piece of inaccessible tree, and after blowing the flame over the head of the victim, performs a series of grotesque gyrations and growls out a string of idiotic gutturals which he probably does not himself remember from one performance to the next.

Then there is also in the mountains not a thousand miles from Pen-Mar an old hag who is known for miles around for her alleged ability to cure the "take-offs." For the enlightenment of the uninformed it may be explained that the "take-off" is described by the hardy mountain women as a malady which attacks children. As one woman said: "When it gets a young one, the child jest gets droopy and won't eat and it keeps on gettin' po'rer and po'rer until it dies, unless you have a 'pow-wow.'"

Invoking the Spirits

A "pow-wow" is explained to mean the act of invoking the alleged supernatural powers. There is not so much secrecy in this rite as in that of the "fire-blower," but it is just as great a humbug and has just as much idiotic tomfoolery.

When the mother of the child with the "take offs" makes her first visit to the old hag who claims to cure them, she is given a small quantity of flour, which she is told to take home and bake into a large loaf of bread. In the meantime the magician mumbles something supposed to be an invocation of some kind of spirits other "moonshine," and then the mother is told to "bring the little dear again next week."

"Trying for it" is the technical term applied to the rite of curing the "take-offs," and while mamma is home baking a big loaf of bread, the old hag is supposed to be "trying for" the child. When mother and child return for the second visit (if the victim has not passed to the great beyond) the old hag asks first for the bread and then for the child.

With the bread clasped tightly in her arms she bids the mother to follow with the child into her log hut. Then the door and windows are closed and the 'take-offs" artist begins to work.

This consists in breaking a small piece from the loaf of bread and performing inexplicable passes of hands over it. All the time the old hag keeps up an unintelligible incantation that sounds like a broken 59-cent alarm clock. The child is made to swallow the piece of bread and mamma is told to "take dearie home" and that it will be entirely cured in less than a week.

Casting Out A Devil

Sometimes it is, but more often it is not, yet that does not shake the faith of the poor ignorant victims, and if the child is not well one week after having been "tried for," it is the common belief that it has been bewitched. It is an undeniable truth that people in the mountains who attend church, almost every Sunday, actually believe in witchcraft.

When the parents decide that the child did not really have the "take offs," but that it is bewitched, the next move is to break the charm. The modus operandi of this extraordinary feat consists of making the child expectorate in the old tin can, which is secretly hung in the chimney of the house. After that it is wait and watch, and the first person who comes into the house to borrow anything is the evil one who bewitched the child.

The watchers must make no demonstration nor even give the slightest indication of what may be passing in their minds, if they possess any.

No intimation is given to the borrower, then nor thereafter, or what is suspected or rather firmly believed by the parents of the afflicted child. All possible haste, however, is made to inform the official charm dispeller of that immediate vicinity. Often he is a "fire-blower" also.

The breaker of "evil spells" visits the house of the sick child and with a piece of string, supposed to have been charmed for just such an emergency, he measures the child's hands and feet. Then he ties the mystic string to the knob or latch of the door which is most frequently used in the house.

The Deadly Cross-Mark

After this he proceeds in solemn manner to make a cross-mark over every window and door of the house. From the moment his marvelous task is completed, it is believed, the person who bewitched the child will never again enter the premises. Thereby the child is kept from further mischief.

No attempt in any way to injure the alleged witch is ever made, for fear that he may be possessed of power to work more harm. It is enough to be thankful that the spell is broken, but the child does not always recover even after that.

There are men and women in the mountains who are reputed to possess the power of being able to "try for" all manner of ailments. There is no doubt that they "try for" them, but how successful they are any intelligent person can easily guess.

However, it is only for serious cases that these specialists are consulted, for the mountain folks have a score of home remedies for lesser ills. Thus a woman who was reared and still lives in a little foothill hamlet, where she attended public school, and is now a regular attendant at church, made a loud cry for a piece of bacon, as soon as she heard that her little daughter had trod on and run a large carpet tack into her foot. As soon as the woman secured the bacon she stuck the carpet tack into it up to the head.

"Now," she said, "her foot'll get all right."

Not a thing was done to the child except to bind a piece of rag around the foot.

Some months later one of the farm horses ran a big nail in its hoof.

"Quick, get the nail and stick it in the piece of bacon up there, next where the tack's a-stickin'" was her first advice.

When asked how that would help the horse, she said that putting the nails in the greasy bacon prevented them from getting rusty and so they would not irritate the wound and cause inflammation.

Potatoes for Rheumatism

When she was asked whether if she cut her finger with a knife she would stick a piece of court plaster on the knife, she replied that she had never heard of that cure, but she knew that once her father was "took" with a "terribly agony" in his back he took a brass ring and tied it on a string so it hung against the the skin just where the "agony" was and it cured him.

Household remedies of similar character run through the whole gamut of the ludicrous down to the firm belief that if a person steals a potato and carries it secretly in his or her clothing, as the case may be, it would cure and forever ward off rheumatism.

It is not intended to convey the idea that every inhabitant of the Blue Ridge Mountains believes in all or any of these superstitions, but it is a fact that the number who do so forms a surprisingly large percentage.

Probably the most astonishing fact of all is that nearly every one of those who believe in the humbug attends regularly a church where religion is preached nearly every Sunday. What effect this preaching has on the hearers is a question which will not be answered here. J.K.S.[203]

The writer's tone is certainly one of arrogance. It is not as though medical treatment at the time was highly advanced. Despite his claims, I find it hard to believe that a country doctor in the early 20th century would have had any better success in treating serious burns than a typical witch doctor. He would have certainly been far more expensive. As for folk remedies, he certainly picked out the most silly, but traditional and homeopathic remedies have been moderately successful in treating some conditions.

The psychosomatic aspect of it cannot be ignored either. If a person believes that he is likely to get better, either because he was treated by a doctor or a witch doctor, he is in fact more likely to get better. As most illnesses and conditions get better on their own, and early medicine was often times only increased the risk of death, having a witch doctor mumble some words over you was often a better alternative.

Regarding charms, the ones they used certainly seemed less silly, and less expensive, than say those magnetic bracelets so often sold at mall kiosks or the other similarly absurd products that one can find advertised on many television stations late at night. Much of humanity has not advanced much.

Finally, his disbelief that religious people would believe in witchcraft is amusing. People believe all sorts of strange things. Religions, while usually complex and mysterious, carry with them all sorts of strange beliefs, rites, and traditions that would seem troubling to an outsider. To these people both witchcraft and Christianity made sense. To another person, one or both of those belief systems may seem absurd.

An article appearing in the April 4, 1909 edition of *The Sun* titled "A Maryland Uncle Remus And His Tales of Haunts And Spells" by Susan E. Clagett states: "There are many curious things in this Maryland of ours, and not the least among them are the deep-rooted and singular superstitions of the old colored folk."[204] However, she also writes that "[t]his characteristic of the former slaves does not seem to belong to any appreciable extent to the present generation, though the children whose parents were one time slaves, possess in a remarkable degree the fatalism of the old race."[205] Much of Clagett's article is her transcribing black dialogue which is very difficult to read or understand. It appears to offer nothing new to what was previous covered.

There are newspaper accounts from *The Washington Post* and *The Baltimore Sun* of alleged witches in other States being charged with various crimes, generally disturbing the peace. There appear to be no additional accounts of cases like this in the Maryland area during this time period.

An article that appeared in *The Sun* on October 13, 1912 titled "Ghosts, Witches and 'Ha'nts' of the Eastern Shore" states that "No better field for the study of folklore in this country can be found than the Eastern Shore of Maryland, and its traditions, legends, myths and superstitions, if contained in book form, would be a valuable contribution to this fascinating branch of literature."[206] Regarding witches in particular, the reporter wrote:

> Perhaps the most fascinating of all the folklore stories extant at the present day are those of witches and their tricks or "spells." Many sections of the Eastern Shore have their neighborhood witches, and the misfortunes and general "bad luck" of the community are visited upon them.
>
> One man not long ago lost all his horses and had his barn and stables burned because he had incurred the enmity of an unknown witch. In order to break the spell he had to resort to all the methods known to witchcraft. Among the accomplishments of a real witch are the following:
>
> A witch can take a horse from a locked stable and ride it all night, the evidence of this being the witch knots tied in its tail and mane see the next morning.
>
> A witch can turn people into horses, ride on them, and she can also turn herself into any animal she pleases. Hunters tell you their dogs frequently trail and tree witches at night, which takes the form of some animal to avoid detection.
>
> A witch, however, like ordinary mortals, has limitations on her powers. She cannot step over a broomstick if laid across a doorway, and if she sits down in a chair in which a fork has been stuck, she cannot rise as long as the fork stays there. If a witch is about to turn a person into a horse and the sleeper awakes, seizes and

holds the witch, without speaking until daylight, she will assume her proper form.

To kill a witch, draw a picture of her and shoot at it with pieces of silver. Just where the picture is shot the witch will be wounded and if in a vital place she will die.

Persons accustomed to driver on summer evenings have often remarked upon the hot waves of air that strike them at intervals. These are the breath of the witches, according to local belief.[207]

The article again demonstrates the fact that witchcraft itself was often used as a tool against witches. Destroying the image of a person is perhaps one of the oldest forms of witchcraft and is still seen in the dying art of burning someone in effigy. Also, as previously mentioned in this book, many of the accounts of witches acting in a person's bedroom could be explained as nightmares or sleep paralysis.

The last newspaper record of note from the early 20th century period is an advertisement from The *Afro-American*, a Baltimore newspaper that still publishes today. Written and read mainly by Baltimore's African-Americans or black population this ad for a witch doctor in what used to be Baltimore County (now within the borders of Baltimore City) appeared in the classified section on December 30, 1916:

Prof. Levanus
King of Clairvoyants
of Balto. Co., MD

Read your life from cradle to grave without asking a question. The greatest born and most gifted medium the world has ever known, even greater than the greatest of Egypt, India and the far East. Can be consulted daily on all matters of Business, Courtship, Love, and Marriage; Changes, Luck, Advice on Horse Racing, at track or by wire, and all other games. Hours 9 to 9 daily and Sunday. By my advice I remove bad influence and unite the separated. Never fail, no matter what your troubles may be or

what you wish to know Prof. Levanus can help you. No matter if you are hundreds of miles away, readings and advice are
acknowledged by the press and the public to be of the highest
order. If you are going to see a medium, why not see the best.
Prof. Levanus' advice is sought by people of all walks of life. All
invited. None slighted. No business done by mail. Either call
or send a friend. Levanus has read the lives of many great and
famous people both home and abroad. Many mediums of reputation have been developed by Prof. Levanus by advice. Remove
witchcraft spell. Prof. Levanus has united and made happy more
separated couples than any medium in the world. Do you feel
bad, have doctors failed to help you? If so seek the advice of
this gifted medium. Does the world seem against you and the
harder you try the greater your troubles are? If so consult Prof.
Levanus and have your luck and happiness restored. No matter who you have consulted do not despair before consulting
this gifted medium. Knowledge of the present is power for the
future. A word to the wise is sufficient. Now friends common
sense teaches you the man has more power than women to
pull you through the troubles of life. Remember Prof. Levanus
transacts all business at his office. I also sell the 6 and 7 books
of Moses, Egyptian secrets and the witches Dream book. Fees
moderate.

Bring this card with you. no sign. Look for the number. Use side
entrance. 520 Highland avenue, First street Highlandtown, Md.
Take Roland Park car to Eastern avenue and First street. Don't
be mis-directed. Look for Levanus. Phone Wolf 5141-w[208]

Again, one must ask why such a gentleman if he had such powers
isn't more well known today? Why didn't he achieve more in his life?
Did he really believe that he was using witchcraft and spiritualism to
help people or was he just a fraud? Like so much, this is an issue for
speculation. This author could find no further references to Professor
Levanus elsewhere.

Stories about witchcraft, sorcery, and superstition would have
appeared less frequently as the years passed by. Old beliefs slowly died

off as people came to look more and more into the light of science and technology. With the advent of modern medical treatment, radar, and other advances as well as devices such as radio and television to inform the masses about the great strides made through science, strong belief in superstition subsided.

Chapter 7
Concluding Thoughts and Observations

When more recently chatting with two African-American ladies from Maryland's eastern shore, whom this author has known for some time, this author asked them if they knew of any good stories involving ghosts, witches, and other supernatural related events from that part of the State.

One knew a ghost story involving a spirit called Big Liz, but claimed no knowledge of witchcraft superstitions. The other did not know of any witches from Maryland, but told this author about a relative in nearby Virginia, from the Chesapeake area, who also had a reputation for being able to work magic.

This woman, it was said, would give her family members special amulets and tell them to take part in certain rituals when they had to go to court to face criminal charges. It was claimed when the family members followed the directions given they always received beneficial results. Apparently this witch once appeared herself in a Maryland court, on the eastern shore, to speak for a relative who was to be sentenced for some crime. The judge, who had a reputation as a rude man who gave harsh sentences, was extremely deferential to the witch, not knowing her previously or of the fact that she practiced witchcraft, and he gave the relative a much lighter sentence than had been expected. This story was presented to this author as an incontrovertibly true. Lawyers may be tempted to wonder why they went to law school and instead did not study at Hogwarts to better assist their clients.

Apparently the witch also had a dark side and was believed to have poisoned another person in the community who had run afoul of her. She had since passed on, although it is unknown if she had passed her knowledge, whatever that may be, onto another. Traditionally witches passed their skills onto their daughters, if they had any.

Despite this anecdotal evidence, one would be hard pressed to find too many people in Maryland who still hold to the ancient witchcraft beliefs. It is impossible to blame witches for storms when we know so much about meteorology. It is absurd to blame them for disease when medical science can diagnose so many conditions and often provide a cure. But still the myths, superstitions, and legends about witches persist, somewhat, among a few.

That the myths are dying is not necessarily bad. No one would seriously suggest that we want to return to some primitive society where witches are not only blamed for problems, but are also uprooted and killed. No one would seriously suggest that we ignore all that we have learned from science. There is, however, still a desire for some degree of mystery. An explained universe or a universe that is capable of being explained completely is extremely boring and rather depressing.

Thankfully, such a thing is not possible. Our world, our universe, still holds plenty of mystery and will always. It is too complex, too strange, too wild, to fit neatly into a little rational box with a bow on top.

Maryland has always had more than a bit of mystery about it. It has been a home to horror writers, such as Thomas Huff and Edgar Allen Poe, who died on the streets of Baltimore under mysterious circumstances. William Fuld, the inventor of the modern Ouija board was a Baltimorean. Every city, small town, and village has ghost stories associated with it.

A sea monster, Chessie, is even said to inhabit the Chesapeake Bay. And one should not forget the various stories of Goatman, Bigfoot, and the Bunny Man. A man in North Ann Arundel County, Conrad Bladey, drives around spooky artcars that frighten children and adults alike.

Matt Lake in his book *Weird Maryland* has documented many of these strange characters. Surely there is room in Maryland's rich lore for rekindled tales of witches, sorcerers, and conjurers practicing their evil arts during the dark of night. Of course we have those who claim that they are witches today, Wiccans, but they are not the same as traditional witches who are said to have either formed a pact with Satan or who otherwise managed to employ his services.

The love of witchcraft lore and legend should never go beyond the speculative. Certainly Maryland has been fortunate not to have had a history of mass witchcraft prosecutions. Five trials, two convictions, and one execution is not a record to be proud of, but it was nothing compared to what was happening in Europe, or even Salem, where convictions were all but certain and numerous. Maryland authorities did not actively seek out witches nor did judges push for convictions. They had no other agenda, it would seem, but to do justice.

One could argue that the circumstances were different. Witch hysteria typically took off during great periods of social unrest, war, or other turmoil. Maryland had its problems, but there were no devastating events that rocked the entire area. Still in other places, such as Scotland, mass trials took place during relative calm, often at the behest of rulers, such as James VI of Scotland who was obsessed with the subject in the early days of his rule. The Calvert rulers and the men they appointed to oversee Maryland were more level-headed and rational on the subject. They would have believed that witches existed and that their power was real, but were not overly concerned with the subject.

William H Cooke

Maryland's days of witch trials are thankfully long gone. Although much of the history and lore associated with it has sadly faded as well. Hopefully this book plays a small role in rekindling this mainly forgotten part of Maryland's past and traditions.

Endnotes

1   King Hammurabi of Babylon, *Code of Laws*, trans. C.H.W. Johns, (New York: Charles Scribner's Sons, 1903) available at Gutenberg Press http://www.gutenberg.org/files/17150/17150.txt . "If a man weave a spell and put a ban upon a man, and has not justified himself, he that wove the spell upon him shall be put to death.

2   Howard Williams, *The Superstitions of Witchcraft* (London: Longman, Green, Longman, Roberts & Green, 1865), 18 -19, available at http://books.google.com.

3   Ibid.

4   Although it may be possible that witches and shamans paid attention to signs that there was about to be a storm and pretended that they caused it through some ritual.

5   The example of the Pendle witches comes to mind. Despite the academic bias against Wikipedia, this author believes that it is a good resource and will cite to it for more general points. Wikipedia contributors, "Pendle witches," *Wikipedia, The Free Encyclopedia*, http://en.wikipedia.org/w/index.php?title=Pendle_witches&oldid=446321471 (accessed September 18, 2011).

6   Chadwick Hansen, *Witchcraft at Salem* (New York: George Braziller, 1969), 84—86.

7   William H. Cooke, *Justice at Salem: Reexamining the Witch Trials* (Annapolis,Undertaker Press, 2009),36.

8   Michael Dalton, *The Country Justice:CONTAINING THE PRACTICE OF THE Justices of the Peace OUT OF THEIR SESSIONS. GATHERED For the better help of Such JUSTICES of Peace, as have not been much conversant in the Study of the Laws of This REALM (London, William Rawlins and Samuel Raycrose, 1690), 383,* retrieved from the Archives of Maryland Website at http://aomol.net/000001/000153/html/am153—383.html (accessed on September 18, 2011)

9   Williams, *The Superstitions of Witchcraft*, 171—172.

William H Cooke

10   Randolph Greenfield Adams, *Political ideas of the American Revolution:Britannic-American contributions to the problem of imperial organization, 1765 to 1775* (Durham: Trinity College Press, 1922), 97—98, available at http://books.google.com.;

Also consider that Maryland's initial charter expressly states as such "**VII.** And forasmuch as We have above made and ordained the aforesaid now Baron of Baltimore, the true Lord and Proprietary of the whole Province aforesaid, Know Ye therefore further, that We, forges, our Heirs and Successors, do grant unto the said now Baron, (in whose Fidelity, Prudence, Justice, and provident Circumspection of Mind, We repose the greatest Confidence) and to his Heirs, for the good and happy Government of the said Province, free, full, and absolute Power, by the Tenor of these Presents, to Ordain, Make, and Enact Laws, of what Kind soever, according to their sound Discretions whether relating to the Public State of the said Province, or the private Utility of Individuals, of and with the Advice, Assent, and Approbation of the Free-Men of the same Province, or the greater Part of them, or of their Delegates or Deputies, whom We will shall be called together for the framing of Laws, when, and as often as Need shall require, by the aforesaid now Baron of Baltimore, and his Heirs, and in the Form which shall seem best to him or them, and the same to publish under the Seal of the aforesaid now Baron of Baltimore, and his Heirs, and duly to execute the same upon all Persons, for the time being, within the aforesaid Province, and the Limits thereof, or under his or their Government and Power, in Sailing towards Maryland, or thence Returning, Outward bound, either to England, or elsewhere, whether to any other Part of Our, or of any foreign Dominions, wheresoever established, by the Imposition of Fines, Imprisonment, and other Punishment whatsoever; even if it be necessary, and the Quality of the Offence require it, by Privation of Member, or Life, by him the aforesaid now Baron of Baltimore, and his Heirs, or by his or their Deputy, Lieutenant, Judges, Justices, Magistrates, Officers, and Ministers, to be constituted and appointed according to the Tenor and true Intent of these Presents, and to constitute and ordain Judges, Justices, Magistrates and Officers of what kind, for what Cause, and with what Power soever, within that Land, and the Sea of those Parts, and in such form as to the said now Baron of Baltimore, or his Heirs, shall seem most fitting; And also to Remit, Release, Pardon, and Abolish, all Crimes and Offences whatsoever against such Laws, whether before, or after Judgment passed; and to do all and singular other Things belonging to the Completion of Justice, and to Courts, Praetorian Judicatories, and Tribunals, Judicial Forms and Modes of Proceeding, although express Mention thereof in these Presents be not made; and, by Judges by them delegated, to award Process, hold Pleas, and determine in those Courts, Praetorian Judicatories, and Tribunals, in all Actions, Suits, Causes, and Matters whatsoever, as well Criminal as Personal, Real and Mixed, and Praetorian: Which said Laws, so to be published as above-said, We will enjoin, charge, and command, to be most absolute and firm in Law, and to be Kept in those Parts by all the Subjects and Liege-Men of Us, our Heirs, and Successors, so far as they concern them, and to be inviolably observed under the Penalties therein expressed, or to be expressed. So, nevertheless, that the Laws aforesaid be consonant to Reason, and be not repugnant or contrary, but (so far as conveniently may be) agreeable to the Laws, Statutes, Customs, and Rights of this Our Kingdom of England." "Charter of Maryland," *Wikisource, The Free Library,* http://en.wikisource.org/w/index.php?title=Charter_of_Maryland&oldid=2802022 (accessed September 24, 2011).

11   Marion Gibson, *Witchcraft myths in American culture* (New York: Taylor & Francis Group, 2007) , 15. The author asserts that witchcraft was illegal, under different colonial laws, in all English colonies, but was not expressly prohibited in New York or Pennsylvania when they were under Dutch authority.

12   Wikipedia contributors, "Salem witch trials," *Wikipedia, The Free Encyclopedia,* http://en.wikipedia.org/w/index.php?title=Salem_witch_trials&oldid=451203997 (accessed September 20, 2011). One person was pressed to death and at least four people were believed to have died in jail pending the resolution of their cases.

13   The settlers under the leadership of William Claiborne came directly from Virginia.

14   Maryland Department of Nature Resources, "St. Clements Island State Park", http://www.dnr.state.md.us/publiclands/southern/st-clements.asp (accessed on September 19, 2011)

15   Wikipedia contributors, "St. Mary's City, Maryland," *Wikipedia, The Free Encyclopedia*, http://en.wikipedia.org/w/index.php?title=St._Mary%27s_City,_Maryland&oldid=412578784 (accessed September 19, 2011).

16   James Walter Thomas, *Chronicles of colonial Maryland* (Cumberland: The Eddy Press Corporation, 1913), 69—76, available at http://books.google.com.

17   William Thomas Russell, *Maryland; the land of sanctuary: A history of religious toleration in Maryland from the first settlement until the American revolution* (Baltimore: J.H. Furst Company, 1907), 26—33, available at http://books.google.com.

18   John Gottlieb Morris, *The Lords Baltimore*(Baltimore: John Murphy, 1874) , 14, available at http://books.google.com. "Sir George, as we have seen, was appointed as one of the Secretaries of State, in 1619, as successor to Sir Thomas Lake, which place he held until 1624, when he resigned it according to Fuller,(1) for the following reasons: 'He freely confessed to the King that *he was then become a Roman Catholic,* so that he must be wanting in his trust or violate his conscience in discharging his office.' 'This his ingenuity,' adds Fuller, 'so highly affected King James, that he continued him Privy Councillor all his reign, and soon after, created him Lord Baltimore of Baltimore, in Ireland."

19   Ibid., 23—30.

20   Ibid., 23.; Henrietta Maria of France was a Catholic and was concerned about the treatment of Catholics in England;
     Also, see Russell, *Maryland; the land of sanctuary*, 19—20. "We may well believe that Charles I, if left to follow the dictates of his naturally easy-going disposition, would have been averse to persecution. His marriage to Henriette Marie would, moreover, have induced him to measures of justice toward Catholics. But the increasing insolence of the Puritan fanatics, their constant accu-

sations against him of showing favor to his Catholic subjects, induced him to make at least a pretense of enforcing the penal laws. His shifty conduct was the cause of frequent quarrels between himself and the queen, who considered herself the defender of the Catholics."

21 "Charter of Maryland," *Wikisource.*

22 Ibid.

23 Ibid.

24 "Maryland Toleration Act, September 21, 1649, An Act Concerning Religion," Lillian Goldman Law Library, http://avalon.law.yale.edu/18th_century/maryland_toleration.asp.

25 The only reference to a blasphemy trial that this author could find involved a Jewish doctor, Jacob Lumbrozo. His trial was ended, mid-trial, when Oliver Cromwell in England died and the Maryland governor issued a general pardon in Cromwell's honor. Raphael Semmes, *Crime and Punishment in Early Maryland* (Baltimore and London: The Johns Hopkins University Press, 1938), 166—167. If anyone has information about a successful prosecution in Maryland for blasphemy please email the author at bill@williamcooke.com.

26 Andrew White, S.J., "A Brieffe Relation of the Voyage Unto Maryland", *Archives of Maryland Online,* http://www.aomol.net/000001/000552/html/index.html .

27 Ibid, 7, at http://aomol.net/000001/000552/html/am552—7.html .

28 Lewis Webb Wilhelm, *Local Institutions of Maryland* (Baltimore: N. Murray, Publication Agent, Johns Hopkins University, 1885), 41, available at http://books.google.com.

29 William Hand Browne, ed., *Proceedings and Acts of the General Assembly January 1637/8-September 1664* (Baltimore: Maryland Historical Society, 1883), 71, available at http://aomol.net/000001/000001/html/am1—71.html.

30 Ibid., 71—72.

31 Ibid., 158.

32 Ibid.

33 Ibid.

34   Capital Punishment U.K., "Timeline of capital punishment in Britain", http://www.capitalpunishmentuk.org/timeline.html .

35   James Grant, *The Mysteries of All Nations* (Edinburgh, W. Paterson, 1880), 249, available at http://www.gutenberg.org/files/19900/19900-h/19900-h.htm . "James was convinced that the storms which kept him and his queen so long from meeting were the results of diabolical agencies. After his return to Scotland, suspicion fell on a dangerous gang of witches and warlocks at Tranent, and the king resolved to inquire into the whole case, with the laudable design of getting rid of such wicked subjects should he find them guilty. A man named David Seytoun, who held the appointment of deputy bailiff of Tranent, had a young female servant named Geillis Duncan, celebrated among the town's people for her skill in curing diseases. Seytoun, becoming suspicious that she was in league with Satan, questioned her closely without receiving satisfactory answers. Not to be defeated, he first put her to the torture, which he thought he had a right to do in virtue of his office, and then searched her person for devil's marks. One of those sure tokens of witchcraft being found on her throat, she was committed to prison. There she made a full confession, in which many persons were implicated. She admitted that the cures effected by her were brought about by means of witchcraft."

36   Ibid., 519—520.

37   Wallace Notestein, *A History of Witchcraft in England from 1558 to 1718* (Washington: The American Historical Association, 1911), 142—143, available at http://www.gutenberg.org/ebooks/31511 . "It is not, then, without being forewarned that we read Fuller's remarkable statement about the king's change of heart. 'The frequency of such forged possessions wrought such an alteration upon the judgement of King James that he, receding from what he had written in his 'Dæmonology,' grew first diffident of, and then flatly to deny, the workings of witches and devils, as but falsehoods and delusions.' In immediate connection with this must be quoted what Francis Osborne has to say. He was told, he writes, that the king would have gone as far as to deny any such opera-

tions, but out of reasons of state and to gratify the church. Such a conversion is so remarkable that we could wish we had absolutely contemporary statements of it."

38   Grant, *The Mysteries*, 398—399.

39   William Hand Browne, ed., *Proceedings of the Council of Maryland, 1636-1667* (Baltimore: Maryland Historical Society, 1885), 306—307, available at http://aomol.net/000001/000003/html/am3—306.html .

40   Ibid., 307—308, available at http://aomol.net/000001/000003/html/am3—307.html .

41   Russell, *Maryland; the land of sanctuary*, 262.

42   Dr. Lois Green Carr, "St. Mary's City Men's Career Files" (Maryland State Archives), http://www.msa.md.gov/megafile/msa/speccol/sc5000/sc5094/001000/001393/html/sc5094-1393-01.html .

43   Edward D. Neill, *The Founders of Maryland :as Portrayed in Manuscripts, Provincial Records and Early Documents* (Albany: Joel Munsell, 1876), 129, available at http://books.google.com .

44   For example, see Russell, *Maryland: the land of sanctuary*, 557. Citing a different source, the author recorded "Mr. Gladstone says: 'It was in 1649 that the Maryland Act of Toleration was passed, which, however, prescribed the punishment of death for anyone who denied the Trinity. Of the small legislative body which passed it, two-thirds appear to have been Protestants, the recorded numbers being sixteen and eight respectively. The colony was open to the immigration of Puritans and all Protestants, and any permanent and successful oppression by a handful of Roman Catholics was altogether impossible.'"

45   Wikipedia contributors, "Society of Jesus," *Wikipedia, The Free Encyclopedia*, http://en.wikipedia.org/w/index.php?title=Society_of_Jesus&oldid=452108319 (accessed September 25, 2011).

46   Daniel Richard Randall, A Puritan Colony in Maryland (Baltimore: N. Murray, Publication Agent, Johns Hopkins University, 1880), 17, available at http://books.google.com . "William Stone, a Protestant of Northampton County, Virginia, who had, however, for two years been living in Maryland, was commissioned Governor, because, as his commission states, 'our trusty and well-beloved

Win. Stone now or late of Northampton County in Virginia, esquire, hath undertaken in some short time to procure five hundred people of British or Irish descent to come from other places and plant and reside within our said Province of Maryland for the advancement of our colony there.' In August, 1648, Stone took his oath of office with the special clause 'not to molest in particular any Roman Catholic.'"

47   Wikipedia contributors, "John Washington," *Wikipedia, The Free Encyclopedia*, http://en.wikipedia.org/w/index.php?title=John_Washington&oldid=436212620 (accessed September 25, 2011).

48   Maryland State Archives, "Agency History for Provincial Court", at http://guide.mdsa.net/history.cfm?ID=SH5 (accessed on September 25, 2011). "The exact date of the creation of the Provincial Court is unknown; it is likely that it dates from Leonard Calvert's commission as Lieutenant General of the colony in 1637, which gave him the authority to try all cases except those concerning life, member, or freehold. Originally called the County Court, the Provincial Court was modeled after the English county courts. The name change probably occurred sometime between 1640 and 1642, when St. Mary's and Kent counties were created, each with a county court. The Provincial Court had concurrent jurisdiction with the county courts in most matters, served as an appellate court to the county courts, and had original jurisdiction in criminal cases involving life or member and in civil cases with value above a given sum or poundage of tobacco, which varied throughout the court's history."

49   Bernard Christian Steiner, ed., *Proceedings of the Provincial Court, 1658-1662* (Baltimore: Maryland Historical Society, 1922), 327—328, available at http://aomol.net/000001/000041/html/am41—327.html .

50   Wikipedia contributors, "Josias Fendall," *Wikipedia, The Free Encyclopedia*, http://en.wikipedia.org/w/index.php?title=Josias_Fendall&oldid=433726777 (accessed September 25, 2011). Fendall shortly thereafter was involved in an unsuccessful rebellion against the Calvert rule.

51 Steiner, ed., *Proceedings of the Provincial Court, 1658—1662*, 328, available at http://aomol.net/000001/000041/html/am41—328. html .

52 Ibid., 328—329.

53 William Hand Browne, ed., *JUDICIAL AND TESTAMENTARY BUSI-NESSOF THEPROVINCIAL COURT1649/50—1657* (Baltimore: Maryland Historical Society, 1891), 399, available at http://aomol. net/000001/000010/html/am10—399.html .

54 Ibid.

55 Ibid.

56 Ibid.

57 See J. Hall Pleasants and Louis Dow Scisco, eds., *PROCEEDINGS OF THE COUNTY COURT OF CHARLES COUNTY 1658-1666 AND MANOR COURT OF ST. CLEMENT'S MANOR1659-1672* (Baltimore: Maryland Historical Society, 1936), 92, available at http://aomol. net/000001/000053/html/am53—92.html . The Court record states "Thomas Mitchell senior hauinge giuen unto Ellizabeth Atwickes Junior One Kow Calf e Dessires her Marke to be Recorded, beinge Ouerkeeled on the Right Ear and A hole in the left Ear." See Ibid., 66, available at http://aomol.net/000001/000053/ html/am53—66.html "Thomas Mitchell Entereth his marke of Hoggs and Cattle (viz) Cropt on the left Ear with A slit in the Grope And A peece taken out of the uper syde of the right Ear like unto A triangle." Both of these references would suggest that Mitchell was a farmer.

58 Ibid., lv. In the Preface, the editors wrote the following "The interesting case of Joan Mitchell (Michael) involving insinuations of witchcraft and a counter suit for defamation, came up in the Charles County Court on November 14. 1659. *Thomas Mitchell complained to the court that "Mis Hatche ", unquestionably the wife of John Hatch, one of Governor Fendali's Council...*" available at http:// aomol.net/000001/000053/html/am53p—55.html .

59 Ibid., 54—55, available at http://aomol.net/000001/000053/html/ am53—54.html .

60 Ibid., lv, available at http://aomol.net/000001/000053/html/ am53p—55.html .

61 Ibid. liii, available at http://aomol.net/000001/000053/html/am53p—53.html . "References to the clergy or to churches are quite infrequent in these early county records. The Rev. Francis Doughtie, a clergyman of the Church of England, with a strong leaning towards Puritanism, was a minister in Charles County, who stirred up much trouble in both Maryland and Virginia. An interesting sketch of his career in England, Massachusetts, Rhode Island, Virginia,and Maryland, has been written by Louis Dow Scisco (Md. Hist. Mag., 1925, xxiii, pp. 155-162). He had been in Northampton County, Virginia, just before he came to Picki-awaxen in Charles County, Maryland in the late fifties, and re-turned to Virginia shortly before 1663 to take a parish in Rappah-annock County (p. 396). Witchcraft was one of his obsessions. In 1657 he had Barbara Winbrow brought before the Northampton Court on suspicion of witchcraft, but the charge was apparent-ly dropped (Bruce's Institutional History of Virginia, i, 280). In Charles County when Doughtie insinuated that Mrs. Joan Mitch-ell was a witch, he was promptly countered in a suit filed in Sep-tember, 1661, by her for defamation of character, which is more fully discussed later (pp. lv, 139, 142-145, 156). After his return to Virginia he got into a dispute in 1668 with two of his Rappahan-nock vestry on account of his 'abstraceous from chants ", and was apparently obliged to leave that colony (Bruce's Institutional History of Virginia, i, 218-219).'"

62 Russell, *Maryland; the land of sanctuary*, 263. "The Presbyteri-ans also found in Maryland a refuge from persecution. Fran-cis Doughty was probably the first pastor of the first Pres-byterian Church in the Province, into which he came about 1657, arriving there by way of a trail of ejectments and arrest. His seems to have been a stormy career, and the man him-self not particularly remarkable for either prudence or self-control."

63 Norma Tucker, *Colonial Virginians and their Maryland relatives:a genealogy of the Tucker family and also the families of Allen, Blackis-tone, Chandler, Ford, Gerard, Harmor, Hume, Monroe, Skaggs, Smith,*

Stevesson, Stone, Sturman, Thompson, Ward, Yowell, and others (Baltimore: Clearfield Company, Inc, 1994), 27.

64   J. Hall Pleasants and Louis Dow Scisco, eds., *PROCEEDINGS OF THE COUNTY COURT OF CHARLES COUNTY*, 139, available at http://aomol.net/000001/000053/html/am53—139.html .
"Joan Michel verses Francis Doughty Minister in an action of slander Warrant to the Sheriffe &c Ret 24th Sept:

Joan Michell Demands a warrant against Enock Doughtie in an action of Slander Warrant to the Sheriff &c Ret: 24th Sept: Subpenes for ditto Michel in ditto Causa Mis Cage Mary Warring William Potter Hew Neale Subpenes to the Sheriffe &c

Joane Michell demands a warrant against Mr James Walker in an action of Slander Warrant to the Sheriff &c Subpene for ditto Michell in ditto Causa Mary Warring William Potter Mis Beane to testifie in ditto Causa

Joane Michell demands a warrant against Mis Long in an action of [p. 148] slander Warrant to the Sheriffe to Arest &c Ret: 24 Sept: Subpe for ditto Michell in ditto Causa Richard Tarlin and his wife and Francis ferenla to testifie upon oath in ditto Causa Subpenes to the Sheriffe & Ret Ut supra"

65   Ibid., 144—145, available at http://aomol.net/megafile/msa/speccol/sc2900/sc2908/000001/000053/html/am53—144.html .

66   Ibid., 145, available at http://aomol.net/megafile/msa/speccol/sc2900/sc2908/000001/000053/html/am53—145.html .

67   Ibid., 142, available at http://aomol.net/megafile/msa/speccol/sc2900/sc2908/000001/000053/html/am53—142.html .

68   Wikipedia contributors, "Witches' mark," *Wikipedia, The Free Encyclopedia,* http://en.wikipedia.org/w/index.php?title=Witches%27_mark&oldid=446262621 (accessed September 25, 2011).

69   Ibid., J. Hall Pleasants and Louis Dow Scisco, eds., *PROCEEDINGS OF THE COUNTY COURT OF CHARLES COUNTY*, 142—143, available at http://aomol.net/megafile/msa/speccol/sc2900/sc2908/000001/000053/html/am53—142.html .

70 Atwood S. Barwick, transc., *Somerset County Judicial Records,
    1687-1689* (Annapolis: Maryland State Archives, 1999), 77,
    available at http://aomol.net/megafile/msa/speccol/sc2900/
    sc2908/000001/000091/html/am91—77.html
    Samuell Collins plt agt: Sumrsett County Ss John Robbins of this
    County Cordwinder & Jno: Robbins & uxor defts Catherin his
    wife were attached to answer unto Samuell Collins of the said
    County Bricklayer in an action of Slander ~ ~ ~ And Whereupon
    the plt: by his Attourny James Sangster comes & sayes that The
    deft: Especially the Above said Catherin hath most Wickedly &
    Malitiously At Severall times calumniated defamed & slandered
    the said plt: as Specially in reporting & perswadeing severall of
    the good people of this County that the plts: wife is a witch
    which At Severall times She did report in the yeare 1687 & more
    particularly upon the Twelfth day of December last past At the
    house of the said defts: She did advise Henry Ledbury of This
    County planter not to buy any Living Creature of the plt: for said
    the said Catherin She will bewitch them & it will never Trive for
    she is a Witch & she would take her oath That the plts: wife was
    a witch likewise upon the 16th: day of Aprill last among Other
    discourses concerning the plts: Wife the said Catherin said to
    Joseph Staton that the plts Wife was a witch & she would prove
    it soe that the plts: doth declare that the said John Robbins &
    Catherin his wife hath not Only Malitiously Slandered & defamed
    the plts: good name but hath induced Severall of the inhabitants
    of this province to creditt and believe her Slanders whereby the
    plts: wifes life may be endangered & Comerce and dealeing taken
    away from the plt: as will appeare more full by Evidence the plt:
    Sayes—he is damnified & hath Loss to the value of Two hundred
    pounds Sterling & thereupon brings his Suite Sangster pro quer
    pledges de pross John Doe
    Evidences Richard Alford Richd: Roe
    Joseph Staten James Taylor &
    Grant Staten part of plt his wife pr: deft
    Henry Sodbury Walter Mc:henery
    Abigall Coster

71   Ibid.

72   Ibid.

73   Ibid. And the said John Robbins by his Attourny Thomas Poole cometh & defendeth the force & injury of the plt: & Saith that his Action he ought not to have for that he never did Slander the plts: wife as in manner & forme declared

74   Ibid. Upon which came both parties by their Attournies aforesaid & by Mutuall consent put Themselves to the judgment of this Court Whereupon it is this day to witt the 12th: day of September as aforesaid considered by This Court that the aforesaid John Robbins pay unto the said Samuell Collins Two-hundred pounds of Tobacco with cost &a

And it is further Ordered by this Court that the said John Robbins & Catherin his wife make their personall appeareance next Court & in the interim to be of the good behaviour Towards all his lordpps good people & especially towards Samuell Collins & his wife &a

75   Francis Neal Parke, "Witchcraft in Maryland," *Maryland Historical Magazine*, December 1936, 271.

76   Ibid., 295.

77   Ibid.

78   Ibid., 295—296.

79   Ibid., 296.

80   Ibid.

81   Ibid., 296—297.

82   See Rebecca L. Logan, "Witches and Poisoners in the Colonial Chesapeake" (PhD diss., The Union Institute, 2001), 244, note regarding page 122. This states that Thomas Burford, who as Attorney General of Maryland, prosecuted at least two witchcraft cases had a copy of this book among his property when he died in 1686;

Semmes, *Crime and Punishment*, 36;

William Hand Browne, ed., *PROCEEDINGS AND ACTSOF THEGeneral Assembly of Maryland OCTOBER 1678—NOVEMBER 1683* (Bal-

timore: Maryland Historical Society, 1889), 70, available at http://
aomol.net/megafile/msa/speccol/sc2900/sc2908/000001/000007/
html/am7—70.html.

"For the Administracon of Justice in and Regulation of the County
Courtes Bee itt Enacted by the Right Honble the Lord Proprietary by & wth the aduice & consent of the upper & Lower houses
of this present Generall Assembly and the Authority of the same
that the Statute bookes of England to these times named Keebles
abridgements of the Statutes & Daltons Justice of the Peace be
bought by the Justices of the Peace or Comissioners of the severall County Courtes at the Charge of the Respective Countyes
to be kept in their severall County Courtes that the Justices and
officers of the said Courtes and others may haue Recourse to
the same as they shall have occasion & that the said Justices of
the said Courtes doe purchase and procure the same by the first
day of January in the yeare of our Lord one thousand six hundred
seventy & Nyne...."

83 See Logan, "Witches and Poisoners", 206. Logan came to the
    same conclusion after comparing parts of an earlier edition, that
    she was able to obtain, to the 1690 edition and could not find a
    difference.

84 Dalton, *The Country Justice,* 383, available at http://aomol.net/
    megafile/msa/speccol/sc2900/sc2908/000001/000153/html/
    am153—383.html .

85 Ibid., 261, available at http://aomol.net/000001/000153/html/
    am153—261.html . "Also where the matter is to be tried by Wit-
    nesses only, it is fit there be two Witnesses at the least (except
    where the Statute doth expresly allow the oath and testimony of
    one Witness.) And so was the opinion of Mr. *Brook,* that in such
    case there ought to be two Witnesses at the least; and agreeable
    thereto also is the Book and Word of God, *Matth.* 18. 16. 2 *Cor.*
    13. *Ps.* 12.*a.* Otherwise it is where the Trial is by a Jury of twelve
    Men, there one Witness sufficeth, yea, there many times Wit-
    nesses are not necessary. See 1 *Plo.* 12. *a.*";
    Also, see Cotton Mather, *The wonders of the invisible world:being
    an account of the tryals of several witches lately executed in New*

England (London: John Russell Smith, 1862), 34, available at http://books.google.com . "It is not requisite, that so *'palpable Evidence of Conviction* should here come in, as 'in other more sensible matters; 'tis enough, if there be 'but so much *circumstantial* Proof or Evidence, as the 'Substance, Matter, and Nature of such an abstruse Mystery 'of Iniquity will well admit.' [*I suppose lie means, tliat whereas in other Crimes we look for more direct proofs, in this there is a greater use of consequential ones.]*"

86   Dalton, *The Country Justice*, 383—384, available at http://aomol.net/000001/000153/html/am153—383.html .

87   Ibid., 384, available at http://aomol.net/000001/000153/html/am153—384.html .

88   Ibid.

89   Ibid.

90   Mather, *The Wonders*, 30. "*If a* Fellow-Witch, *or* Magician, *give Testimony of any Person to be a* Witch; *this indeed is not sufficient for Condemnation; but it is a fit Presumption to cause a strait Examination.*"—quoting Perkins on the subject.

91   See Increase Mather, *CASES of Conscience Concerning Evil Spirits Perforating MEN; WITCHCRAFTS, Infallible Proofs of Guilt in such as are Accused with that CRIME* (London: John Russell Smith, 1862), 255, available on http://books.google.com. Originally printed in 1693 in Boston. Mather wrote "I declare and testifie, that to take away the Life of any one, meerly because a *Spectre* or Devil, in a bewitched or possessed Person does accuse them, will bring the Guilt of innocent Blood on the Land, where such a thing shall be done: Mercy forbid that it should, (and I trust that as it has not it never i will be so) in *New-England*. What does such an Evidence amount unto more than this: Either such an one did afflict such an one, or the Devil in his likeness, or his Eyes were bewitched." There was great concern that innocent people were being convicted and that those convictions rested solely or mainly on so-called spectral evidence (which was the case). Mather expressed the sound opinion that this was an injustice.

92   Ibid.

93   Dalton, *The Country Justice,* 385, available at http://aomol. net/000001/000153/html/am153—385.html .

94   As quoted in Mather, *The Wonders,* 34.

95   See Margaret Alice Murray, *The witch-cult in Western Europe* (Oxford: Clarendon Press, 1921), 16, available at http://www. gutenberg.org/ebooks/20411 . A controversial book, but well-researched, Murray wrote "Still another objection is that the evidence was always given under torture, and that the wretched victims consequently made reckless assertions and accusations. In most of the English and many of the Scotch trials legal torture was not applied; and it was only in the seventeenth century that pricking for the mark, starvation, and prevention of sleep were used. Even then there were many voluntary confessions given by those who, like the early Christian martyrs, rushed headlong on their fate, determined to die for their faith and their god."

96   Ibid.

97   Dalton, *The Country Justice,* 385, available at http://aomol. net/000001/000153/html/am153—385.html .

98   Ibid.

99   Ibid., 385—386, available at http://aomol.net/000001/000153/ html/am153—385.html .

100 I and others have speculated on the witchcraft trials in Salem. See my previously cited book *Justice at Salem.*

101 Wikipedia contributors, "Province of Maryland," *Wikipedia, The Free Encyclopedia,* //en.wikipedia.org/w/index.php?title=Province_ of_Maryland&oldid=450590682 (accessed October 2, 2011).

102 Maryland Archives, "Senate", http://mdarchives.us/msa/ mdmanual/05sen/html/senf.html . "*17th Century.* The Senate of Maryland originated as the Upper House of the General Assembly, formally distinguished from the Lower House in 1650. This division provided 'for the more convenient dispatch of the busines therein to bee consulted of' (Chapter 1, Acts of 1650). Since the Upper House consisted of the governor and his council, all of whom held close personal and political ties with the Lord Proprietary, the separation of the two Houses gave Lord Baltimore control of the legislature. Frequently, the political interests of the

Upper House came in conflict with those of the Lower House which advocated a popular government and more legislative influence."

103 There are no surveys from the period that give us any idea of the percentage of Catholics , Anglicans, or others. The statement is not unreasonable speculation.

104 Cooke, *Justice*, 83.

105 While there were democratic (or what passed as democratic) elections for the lower house, as previously demonstrated the upper house was appointed by the governor, as were the judges, so the people had very little control over their government.

106 J. Hall Pleasants, ed., *ARCHIVES OF MARYLAND XLIX PROCEEDINGS OF THE PROVINCIAL COURT OF MARYLAND 1663—1666* (Baltimore: Maryland Historical Society, 1932), 486, available at http://aomol.net/megafile/msa/speccol/sc2900/sc2908/000001/000049/html/am49—486.html .
"The Grand Jury Came into Court, & brought These Bills.Jacob Negro Inditemt for murther, Billa VeraThomas Courtny—Ignoramus. Elizabeth Bennett for Witch &c: Ret, not prsentable."

107 Historic St. Mary's City , "Calvert Family Tree", http://www.st-maryscity.org/history/Calvert%20Family%20Tree.html .

108 Pleasants, ed., *Proceedings of the Provincial Court of Maryland 1663—1666*, 508, available at http://aomol.net/megafile/msa/speccol/sc2900/sc2908/000001/000049/html/am49—508.html .
"John Ellis, Elizabeth Bennet, & Thomas Courtney Cleared by Pnoclamãon."

109 William Hand Browne, *PROCEEDINGS AND ACTS OF THE GENERAL ASSEMBLY OF MARYLAND APRIL 1666—JUNE 1676* (Baltimore: Maryland Historical Society, 1884), 425, available at http://aomol.net/megafile/msa/speccol/sc2900/sc2908/000001/000002/html/am2—425.html

110 Ibid., 425—426, available at http://aomol.net/megafile/msa/speccol/sc2900/sc2908/000001/000002/html/am2—425.html .

111 Wikipedia contributors, "Prince George's County, Maryland," *Wikipedia, The Free Encyclopedia,* http://en.wikipedia.org/w/index.

William H Cooke

php?title=Prince_George%27s_County,_Maryland&oldid=
453453426 (accessed October 3, 2011).

112 In the event that this website is not available, the reference
to the Maryland State Archives is—"PROVINCIAL COURT
(Criminal Record) 1683-1706 S547", http://guide.mdsa.net/series.
cfm?action=viewSeries&ID=S547 .

113 Maryland Provincial Court, *Provincial Court (Criminal Record)
1683—1706*, 27 (of the PDF file), available at http://www.jus-
ticeatsalem.com/earlymdcourtrecords.pdf .

114 Ibid., 36.; Parke, "Witchcraft in Maryland," 283.

115 Ibid.,; Ibid., 283-284.

116 Prince George's County Department of Parks and Recreation,
"Mount Calvert Historical and Archaeological Park", http://www.
pgparks.com/Things_To_Do/Nature/Mount_Calvert_Histori-
cal_and_Archaeological_Park.htm .

117 Wikipedia contributors, "Witch bottle," *Wikipedia, The Free Encyclopedia*, http://en.wikipedia.org/w/index.php?title=Witch_bottle&
oldid=419944172 (accessed October 9, 2011).

118 Rebecca Morehouse, "Witch Bottle," Maryland Department
of Planning, Jefferson Patterson Park & Museum, August 2009,
http://www.jefpat.org/CuratorsChoiceArchive/2009CuratorsCh
oice/Aug2009-WitchBottle.html .

119 Logan, "Witches and Poisoners". This was previously cited.

120 When discussing my work on this topic while at an event at a
bookstore I explained the story of Rebecca Fowler to a middle
aged woman who seemed reasonably intelligent. I told her that
Fowler had been an indentured servant and when I said that she
was hanged for witchcraft, the horrified woman asked "because
she was black?" She apparently was unaware that indentured servants could be, and usually were, white. I'm sure that most people
realize this, but for the benefit of anyone who has not figured it
out, Fowler was in fact a white English woman.

121 Logan, "Witches and Poisoners", 100—102, 233- 234; Logan
sites Maryland Patent Book Q, p. 30 as the primary source.

122 Ibid., 102, 233.

123 Ibid., 106, 236.

124 Ibid., 107, 236.

125 Ibid., 109, 238. Logan cites to the Maryland Patent Book 17, pages 145 and 312 and the Maryland Will Book 4, pages 39-40. This author has visited the Maryland Archives and has ordered scans of the primary resources. They have not yet been received. The Archives is a great resource, but they are extremely slow with everything. My personal website http://www.falklands.org will have a link to the book's website when it is created and the documents as well as other items, including pictures, should be available for free.

126 Ibid., 111—112; The reference to the Maryland Will Book 4, p 39-40 is cited.

127 Ibid., 111—112, 239—240; Logan cites Maryland Paten book 22, p. 20 and Patent Book S.D.#A, p. 524. Again, this author is waiting for PDFs of the original documents from the Archives, which will be placed online.

128 Ibid., 112—114; 240—241.

129 Ibid.

130 Ibid., 115.

131 Ibid., 123, 244.

132 Maryland Provincial Court, *Provincial Court (Criminal Record) 683—1706*, 51—52 (of the PDF file), available at http://www.justiceatsalem.com/earlymdcourtrecords.pdf . Parke, "Witchcraft in Maryland," 285—286.

133 Ibid.

134 Logan, "Witches and Poisoners," 126—127, 245—246; Logan cites the Maryland Will Book 5, p.50.; Logan also cites and this author has confirmed—Elizabeth Merritt, ed., *ARCHIVES OF MARYLANDLX VIIPROCEEDINGSOF THEPROVINCIAL COURT OF MARYLAND1677- 1678COURT SERIES(12)* (Baltimore: Maryland Historical Society, 1956), 131 available at http://aomol.net/megafile/msa/speccol/sc2900/sc2908/000001/000067/html/am67—131.html , 235 available at http://aomol.net/megafile/msa/speccol/sc2900/sc2908/000001/000067/html/am67—235.html .

135 Logan, "Witches and Poisoners," 127—128, 246—247; In regards to the murder by Indians, Logan cites and this author has

reviewed—William Hand Browne, ed., *PROCEEDINGS OF THE COUNCIL OF MARYLAND* (Baltimore: Maryland Historical Society, 1896), 178—179, available at http://www.msa.md.gov/megafile/msa/speccol/sc2900/sc2908/000001/000015/html/am15—178.html .

136   Logan, "Witches and Poisoners," 133.

137   Ibid., 135.

138   Ibid., 133.

139   Ibid., 133, 248.

140   Ibid., 134, 248. Logan directs the reader to the Parke article that lists all the parties involved in the case, including jurors. The PDF uploaded to http://www.justiceatsalem.com/earlymdcourtrecords.pdf also supports this.

141   Ibid., 134.

142   Ibid., 135.

143   Ibid.

144   Ibid.

145   Conway Whittle Sams and Elihu Samuel Riley, *The bench and bar of Maryland:a history 1634 to 1901, Volume 1* (Chicago: The Lewis Publishing Company, 1901), 96, available at http://books.google.com .

146   Logan, "Witches and Poisoners," 122, 244. Logan appears to cite to another thesis, Day, 138, which this author believes is *A social study of lawyers in Maryland, 1660-1775* by Alan F. Day. If additional information is brought to light on this issue after publication the book's website will be updated with it.

147   For example, see Cooke, *Justice*, 73—77.

148   Wikipedia contributors, "Annapolis, Maryland," *Wikipedia, The Free Encyclopedia,* //en.wikipedia.org/w/index.php?title=Annapolis,_Maryland&oldid=454356478 (accessed October 9, 2011).

149   Parke, "Witchcraft in Maryland," 287—288. A scan of this document has been ordered by this author and will be available on the website when it arrives from the Maryland Archives.

150   Wikipedia, "Province," http://en.wikipedia.org/w/index.php?title=Province_of_Maryland&oldid=454755172 (accessed October 9, 2011).

151   Parke, "Witchcraft in Maryland," 288.

152 Ibid., 289.

153 Benjamin Ofle Tayloe, *In Memoriam* (Washington: Spero Meliora, 1872), 360, available at http://books.google.com .

154 Hester Dorsey Richardson, *Side-lights on Maryland history:with sketches of early Maryland families, Volume II* (Baltimore, Williams and Wilkins Company, 1913), 17.

155 C. Ashley Ellefson. *William Bladen of Annapolis, 1673?-1718: "the most capable in all Respects" or "Blockhead Booby"?*. (Cortland, NY: 2007), 166—167.

156 James Thos. Law, ed., *THE ECCLESIASTICAL STATUTES AT LARGE, EXTRACTED FROM THE GREAT BODY OF THE STATUTE LAW, AR-RANGED UNDER SEPARATE HEADS, Volume V* (London: WILLIAM BENNING AND Co, 1847), 418—419, available at http://books.google.com .

157 Wikipedia contributors, "William Kilty," *Wikipedia, The Free Encyclopedia*, http://en.wikipedia.org/w/index.php?title=William_Kilty&oldid=361115300 *(accessed October 9, 2011)*.

158 William Kilty, *A report of all such English statutes as existed at the time of the first emigration of the people of Maryland:and which by experience have been found applicable to their local and other circumstances; and of such others as have since been made in England or Great-Britain, and have been introduced, used and practised, by the courts of law or equity; and also all such parts of the same as may be proper to be introduced and incorporated into the body of the statute law of the state* (Annapolis, Jehu Chandler, 1811), 190.

159 Ibid. Kilty's full note was "Although I have met with no instance of a prosecution under the last part of this statute, yet it may have been in force with the first part, which certainly extended to the province in its beneficial effects in repealing the statute I James I, Ch. 12, which, strange as it may seem, had been in use. It will appear by the commissions to the judges, that they were to determine concerning *witchcraft*, burglary, felony, murder, &c. and the charges to the grand juries were to the same effect, until a short period: after the making of this statute.

In 1685 there was an indictment against R. F. for witchcraft, against the form of the statute. There was a special verdict finding the facts, and if, &c. The court took time to consider till the next term. 'Afterwards, &c. the court having advised themselves of, and upon the premises, it is considered by the court, that the said R F. be hanged by the neck, till she be dead,' which was performed the 9th day of October, aforesaid. There were two other cases, one in 1686, and the other in 1712, in which the verdicts were, " not guilty;" but this statute is not considered necessary to be incorporated in the present state of society, and under our constitution even as to the last part; no persons being now found so absurd as to pretend to exercise such witchcraft, &c."

160 Wikipedia contributors, "Moll Dyer," *Wikipedia, The Free Encyclopedia,* http://en.wikipedia.org/w/index.php?title=Moll_Dyer&oldid= 431079718 (accessed October 10, 2011).

161 Ibid.

162 Ibid.

163 Rebecca Key, "A notice of some of the first buildings with notes of some of the early residents," in *Maryland historical magazine, Volume 14,* eds., William Hand Browne and Louis Henry Dielman (Baltimore: Maryland Historical Society., 1919), 268, available at http://books.google.com .

164 Ibid., 267.

165 Ibid., 268.

166 David Ridgely, ed., *Annals of Annapolis, comprising sundry notices of that old city from the period of the first settlements in its vicinity in the year 1649, until the war of 1812* (Baltimore: Cushing & brother, 1841), 119, available at http://books.google.com .

167 Key, "A notice," 259.

168 Aubrey C. Land, ed., *ARCHIVES OF MARYLAND LXXI JOURNAL AND CORRESPONDENCEOF THE STATE COUNCIL OF MARYLAND (9) JOURNAL OF THE STATE COUNCIL 1784-1789* (Baltimore: Maryland Historical Society, 1970), 171, available at http://aomol. net/megafile/msa/speccol/sc2900/sc2908/000001/000071/html/ am71—171.html .

169 Colonial Dames of America, *Ancestral records and portraits:a compilation from the archives of Chapter 1* (Baltimore: The Grafton Press, 1910), 517, available at http://books.google.com .

"Captain John Kilty, was born 1756, and died May 27, 1811. He was Captain of the first regiment of Light Dragoons, 1783, with a record of six years and eight months' active service, in the war of the Revolution. He was a brother of Chancellor William Kilty, of Maryland, who was first Chief Justice of the District of Columbia."

170 Freaknfuzz, "The ghosts of Primrose Hill," http://ghostlyfreak-nfuzz.wordpress.com/2009/10/24/the-ghosts-of-primrose-hill/ .

171 Prentiss Ingraham, *Land of legendary lore: sketches of romance and reality on the eastern shore of the Chesapeake* (Easton, MD: The Gazette publishing house, 1898), 93—94, available at http://books.google.com .

172 "On the Eastern Shore, *McBride's magazine, Volume 18* (Philadelphia: J.B. Lippincott and co., 1876), 472, available at http://books.google.com .

173 Elias Jones, *History of Dorchester County, Maryland* (Baltimore: Williams & Wilkins, 1902), 194—195, available at http://books.google.com .

174 Cooke, *Justice*, 41—42.

175 For a good discussion of this topic see: Chadwick Hansen, *Witchcraft at Salem* (New York: George Braziller, 1969), 10 -11, 43, 71, 86, 181, 201.

176 Tom Peete Cross, "Witchcraft in North Carolina," *Studies in Philology*, Vol. XVI, Number 3, (1919), 283, available at http://books.google.com .

177 Ibid., 273.

178 Ibid., 278—279.

179 Ibid., 287.

180 Ibid., 234.

181 Ibid., 284—285.

182 "The March of Mind," *The Baltimore Sun*, March 3, 1838.

183 "City Court, Saturday, March 30th, 1839," *The Baltimore Sun*, April 1, 1839.

184 Classified Ad, *The Baltimore Sun*, April 24, 1860, pg. 3.

185 "Rowdyism in South Carolina," *The Baltimore Sun*, August 10, 1872, pg 1.

186 "A Murderous Monomaniac," *The Washington Post*, July 28, 188, pg. 1.

187 Wikipedia contributors, "Washington, D.C.," *Wikipedia, The Free Encyclopedia*, http://en.wikipedia.org/w/index.php?title=Washington,_D.C.&oldid=454118436 (accessed October 11, 2011).

188 "A Negro and a Hoodoo Doctor," *The Washington Post*, September 6, 1885, pg. 2.

189 Although if you will permit an off-topic remark, the victim in this case doesn't seem any more gullible than the people today who assume that the Federal government can spend as much as it wants because it prints its own money, as if that won't eventually cause serious inflation. Money is never free.

190 "Bits of Local News," *The Washington Post*, September 10, 1885, pg 4.

191 "Witchcraft and Spells," *The Baltimore Sun*, November 30, 1886, pg. 6.

192 "A Place for the Hoodoo," *The Washington Post*, September 21, 1890, pg 4.

193 "Article 13—No Title," *The Washington Post*, January 4, 1891, pg 4.

194 "Capt. Russ as a Hoodoo," *The Washington Post*, August 5, 1891, pg 6.

195 "Thinks it is a Hoodoo; Influence of Fred Simpson over young Estella Lucas; Explanations by her aunt; The Latter's Belief that an Attempt Had Been Made to Poison Her—A Sensation Among the Colored People of Southwest Washington," *The Washington Post*, August 15, 1891, pg. 8.

196 "Hoodoos for a hobby; Superstitions Prevalent Among Some Members of the Police Force. Officer Dyer's Observations; Connection a Call for the Patrol Wagon with a Black Cat—Crap-Shooters and Wife-Beaters-Lieut. McCathran's Cigar a Jonah," *The Washington Post*, November 1, 1891, pg. 15.

197 "Trouble with Reptiles, An Athletic Negro Crank Storms the White House. Wanted His Hoodoo Off," *The Washington Post*, July 2, 1893, pg. 5.

198 Wikipedia contributors, "Phencyclidine," *Wikipedia, The Free Encyclopedia,* http://en.wikipedia.org/w/index.php?title=Phencyclidine&oldid=455389792 (accessed October 16, 2011).

199 "Maryland Folklore," *The Baltimore Sun*, August 25, 1899, pg 7.

200 "Persecuted as a Witch" *The Baltimore Sun,* October 11, 1901.

201 "Says He Couldn't Be Good," *The Baltimore Sun*, August 5, 1902, pg 12.

202 "A Perennial Nuisance," *The Baltimore Sun*, October 15, 1908, pg 4.

203 "Blue Ridge Mountaineers Who Still Believe in Witchcraft, Magic and Devils," *The Baltimore Sun*, January 31, 1909, pg 13.

204 Susan E. Clagett, "A Maryland Uncle Remus And His Tales of Haunts And Spells," *The Baltimore Sun*, April 4, 1909.

205 Ibid.

206 "Ghosts, Witches and 'Ha'nts' of the Eastern Shore," *The Baltimore Sun*, October 13, 1912.

207 Ibid.

208 Classified Ad, *The Afro-American*, December 30, 1916.

Made in the USA
Middletown, DE
08 August 2020